CLASSIFIED

UCD WOMEN'S CENTER

CLASSIFIED

How To Stop
Hiding Your Privilege
and Use It
For Social Change

UCD WOMEN'S CENTER

Karen Pittelman &
Resource Generation
Illustrated by
Molly Hein

Design by Katya Popova

Published by Soft Skull Press
55 Washington Street, Suite 804
Brooklyn, NY 11201
www.softskull.com

Distributed by Publishers Group West
www.pgw.com | 800.788.3123

Library of Congress Cataloging-in-Publication Data
Pittelman, Karen.
Classified : how to stop hiding your privilege and start using it for
social change / by Karen Pittelman.
      p. cm.
   ISBN-13: 978-1-933368-08-5 (alk. paper)
1. Social values—United States. 2. Wealth—Social aspects—United States.
3. Young adults—United States—Attitudes. 4. Social action—United
 States. 5. Social justice—United States. 6. Social change—United States.
 I. Title.

HN90.M6P57 2005
305.242'086'21—dc22
2005019655

Printed in Canada

For Yoav.
And for Alison,
the missing name on
the cover of this book.

contents

The first half of the book is about understanding privilege:

The second half of the book is about taking action:

preface

Resource Generation (RG) is a national non-profit organization that supports and challenges young people with wealth to use their resources for social change. As staff, we've learned that this sentence, simple as it seems, raises a bunch of questions right up front. What do you mean by wealth? By social change? What do you actually do? Why do you do it? So we figured it was essential to start off with answers to some frequently asked questions.

how do you define "young people with wealth"?

"Young people" basically refers to ages 15 to 35, though we're not checking anyone's ID at the door.

Defining what wealth means is tougher. One way to do it is through statistics. For example, in 2001, the wealthiest 10 percent of U.S. residents had over $119,000 in household income or over $736,000 in household assets.*

While statistics can provide a quick definition for those who have earned or inherited money, we also use the word wealth to stand for the experiences of privilege that come with class status, regardless of current income. This means our definition of wealth includes people who have grown up in wealthy families but do not currently have access to any money themselves. Some may inherit later. Some may never inherit. Some may have access to family philanthropy, giving them decision-making power over grants or gifts they might otherwise never be able to make on their own.

RG has always asked that participants make the final definition for themselves whether or not they identify as a young person with wealth.

how do you define "social change"?

We stay pretty broad with our definition of social change, and generally refer to it as a belief in a more just distribution of resources. This isn't because we're unimaginative, but because we want to defer to the visions of current movements for social, economic and environmental justice. An important part of our work is helping people with privilege become more effective participants in social change by listening more and defining less.

what does RG do?

Many young people with wealth feel strongly that the current distribution of resources in the U.S. and in the world is unjust. Yet the knowledge that they are

---

* Based on an analysis of the Federal Reserve's 2001 Survey of Consumer Finances.

a part of the small percentage of people who benefit from this distribution creates a mass of complications and contradictions. It becomes difficult for them to figure out both where they stand and how to take a stand on their beliefs.

RG was founded in 1996 to help young people with wealth make sense of these complications and contradictions. As RG staff, we've seen again and again what a difference this can make in their lives: how it mobilizes people to align their resources with their social change values and to take action as activists and as donors.

how is this work a part of movements for social justice?

We believe that when people with wealth have a deep understanding of their own privilege, they can play an important role in movements for social justice as both participants and funders.

People with wealth can bring needed resources, access and connections to movements. They can talk openly about the ways they've witnessed privilege working and why this grounds their commitment to social change. They can help name some of the destructive power dynamics around wealth and class that often chip away at movements from within. People with wealth can powerfully challenge others with privilege by speaking from a place of shared experience.

However, when people with wealth act without a deep understanding of their privilege, it can undermine their participation. They cannot open up conversations about their connections and resources. They are unable to recognize their own patterns or to challenge others with privilege—leaving those who are the everyday targets of painful power dynamics alone in the role of pointing them out.

RG hopes that by helping people with wealth gain a deeper understanding of their own privilege and by giving them the tools they need to participate in long-term change in new ways, we can be a small part of strengthening movements for social justice.

why focus on class when there are so many other types of privilege that need to be addressed?

The word privilege obviously signifies much more than wealth. The unjust distribution of resources relies on globally interweaving systems of oppression—like racism and sexism—to keep it going. In particular, this book is both grounded in and indebted to anti-racist analyses. However, it is in no way our intention to collapse all systems of oppression into one. In this book we do our best to look at some of the ways these different systems work. Yet we also know we are barely skimming the surface.

We have chosen to focus on privilege through the lens of wealth and class in the United States. These choices are based on our goals and strategies as an organization, not because we feel that there is one type of privilege more important to address than any other. We believe that helping people understand their class privilege is just a starting point for a broader understanding of oppression.

who creates all this stuff at RG?

While RG creates programs and materials specifically for young people with wealth, this stuff is created *by* a cross-class staff. Our analyses and strategies are rooted in the commitment each of us shares to movements for social justice. We bring a whole range of experiences with social change issues to this work, from queer youth organizing to sustainable development to reproductive rights. We also bring a whole range of life experiences with privilege and discrimination, power and oppression—our work together has always drawn its greatest strength from the dialogues this has inspired.

Of course, RG is so much larger than our tiny staff of five. The understanding of power that is at the core of this book grew out of years of collaboration and conversations with our board and with an amazing group of activists, trainers and all-around big-brains. No matter how busy they were, these folks were always willing to take the time to hash out the huge questions with us or give us a loving smack when we were missing the point.

helping people learn about privilege is a nice idea in theory, but how do you actually do it?

How do people learn about their own privilege? It's a long-held truth in social justice movements that anyone trying to learn more about where they're coming from should spend some serious time with those who share similar life experiences. We believe this holds just as true for people with wealth. The best way to start understanding class privilege is to spend time with those who share similar life experiences. This is only a first step on a long road towards cross-class dialogue and taking action for a more just distribution of resources, but we believe it's a crucial one.

This is why the core of RG's work requires bringing young people with wealth together in a way that is both supporting and challenging, where young people can start to find the similarities in their experiences and get a larger picture of how privilege works.

One of the main ways we create this kind of space is by speaking directly to people's lived experiences with privilege. We believe that the most powerful learning grows from people's own observations and first-hand experiences. So while this preface is written as "we, the RG staff," the rest of this book is written as "we, young people with wealth." The truth of that voice comes from hundreds of interviews, one-on-ones and workshops with young people with wealth, as well as years of staff experience.

how can you act so silly when this is serious work?

Another guiding principal in our work is that we do our best to bring in the funny and even a bit of the silly when we can. Talking about class can be a pretty taboo subject in the U.S., which leads most people to keep their experiences with wealth "classified." We find that laughing is often the best way to break the ice and help people find the courage to look at the hard stuff.

We've also learned that understanding privilege has to happen at the level of emotions or it never really happens at all. So we have a style that is heavier on the experiential, storytelling side and much lighter on the statistic-y, academic side. However, we completely rely on the scholars and activists who put the theory and research out there with academic rigor, and would be at a total loss without their work. Many of these authors are listed in the Resource Section, and we also keep an updated reference section on the RG website at www.resourcegeneration.org.

what's the point of this book?

Hopefully we've been able to answer a few of the questions about what led us to create this book and the thought behind it. Now all that's left is to cross our fingers and send this baby out into the world. We hope it will serve its purpose: to help young people with wealth stop hiding their privilege and, instead, start using it to support social change.

—*The RG staff of 2004:*
John, Alison, Hez, Sally and Karen

acknowledgments

------▶ This book is the result of many, many people's brainpower.

First and foremost, thank you to Tracy Hewat, Resource Generation's founder. Tracy authored RG's original resource guide, *Money Talks. So Can We.*, together with Lynne Gerber. Their work was the inspiration for this book.

Thank you to the RG staff, both past and present: Sally Bubier, Alison Goldberg, John Harrison, Hez Norton, Jamie Schweser and Courtney Young. To our past RG fellows: Patrick Cahn, Dan Comstock and Peter Redington. And to everyone who has served on the RG board over the years.

Courtney Young needs to get thanked twice, because before she even joined the staff she conducted over thirty interviews and authored two fabulous booklets for us based on them. (Many of the quotes here were published in an earlier form in those booklets.) Thank you to Meghan Tauck, our other interview goddess, and to Cameron Jordan, Leslie Falconer and Eleonora Frey for the family philanthropy interviews. Thanks to our patient transcribers. Thank you to all our interviewees for sharing their stories and allowing us to share them with others.

Thank you to Richard Nash and everyone at Soft Skull, and to the team who turned this manuscript into a book: Eula Biss, Hannah Bureau, Bryn Canner, Katya Popova, Aviva Rothman-Shore, Naomi Shore and Rita Zilberman.

So many people helped us develop the ideas and the programs at RG that this book grew out of. This isn't even close to everybody: Calvin Allen, Omisade Billie Burney, Tracy Burt, Mahea Campbell, Yee Won Chong, Julio Dantas, Peter Diaz, Anne and Christopher Ellinger, Sarah Feinberg, Tim Freundlich, Sharna Goldseker, Adria Goodson, Jethro Heiko, Julie Johnson McVeigh, Heetan Kalan, Charles Knight, Melissa Kohner, Autumn Leonard, Nicole Levine, Cheryl Linear, Lily Mendez-Morgan, Heather Miller, Emily Nepon, Trinh Nguyen, Susan Ostrander, David Perrin, Charlotte Redway, Page Rossiter, Edie Rubinowitz, Rachel Rybaczuk, Malika Sanders, Rusty Stahl, Lisa Tracy, Christian Willauer and Prentice Zinn.

A special thank you to everyone who took even more time out of their lives to read drafts of this book for RG: Alejandro Amezcua, Kenny Bailey, Deahdra Butler-Henderson, Oona Coy, Martin Evans, Kalpana Krishnamurthy, Jenny Ladd, Carole Pittelman, Carolyn Sweeney, Naomi Swinton, Noy Thrupkaew, Stephanie Yang and Felice Yeskel. And to Liz Werner, the inspiration for the "classified" theme.

Thank you to all of the organizations whose work with people with wealth have inspired and informed our own, including: Access Strategies Foundation, Active Element Foundation, Changemakers, Class Action, Emerging Practioners in Philanthropy, the network of Funding Exchange funds, The Inheritance Project, National Committee for Responsive Philanthropy, National Network of Grantmakers, Responsible Wealth, Southern Partners Fund, Third Wave Foundation, Tides Foundation, and United for a Fair Economy. And to the groups who co-founded RG: Boston Women's Fund, Haymarket People's Fund, More than Money, Peace Development Fund, United Black and Brown Fund, and Youth on Board.

Thank you to the People's Institute for Survival and Beyond for their "Undoing Racism" training, and to the Western States Center and the Peace Development Fund for their "Dismantling Racism" training—these trainings deeply influenced this book.

Thank you to all the sponsors who provided us with the funding we needed to make this book a reality: Progressive Asset Management, Appalachian Community Fund, Astraea Lesbian Foundation For Justice, Bread and Roses Community Fund, Boston Common Asset Management, Calvert Foundation, Changemakers, Chinook Fund, Crossroads Fund, EcoLogic Development Fund, The Fund for Santa Barbara, Fund for Southern Communities, the Funding Exchange, The Global Fund for Women, Haymarket People's Fund, Investors' Circle, MADRE, Ms. Foundation for Women, The New World Foundation, NorthStar Asset Management, North Star Fund, Peace Development Fund, Proteus Fund, Rudolph Steiner Foundation, San Diego Foundation for Change, Southern Partners Fund, Third Wave Foundation, Threshold Foundation, Tides Foundation, The Twenty-First Century Foundation, Trillium Asset Management, Wisconsin Community Fund, and Women Donors Network.

Karen would also like to thank: Yoav, my heart. Deahdra and everyone at Chahara Foundation. My friends, for keeping me laughing and trying their best to keep me sane. My family for their love and their patience with the path I chose. John and Alison for *everything*. And Molly, the best illustrator a girl could dream of—thanks for all the pie.

Molly would like to thank: Dan Griffin, my boo, the first person to make me laugh about money. Liz Werner, Eula Biss, Masami Kawai, and Jonna Shelomith, my fierce allies and best friends. Lisa Gimbel, Lisa Hinton, Wil Sands, Pari Zutshi and Cassaundra Adler, my dialogue and feedback crew. Mary Bombardier, Jose Colon and El Arco Iris, my patient teachers. Ethan Hein, for lending comic book expertise and big brother seal-of-approval. My parents Karen Hein and Ralph Dell, for lovingly supporting me and persevering in the challenge of explaining to people what exactly it is that I do. William Upski Wimsatt, who dragged my ass kicking and screaming to RG in the first place. And special thanks to Karen Pittelman and Alison Goldberg, for giving me access to your big brains. I would also like to thank my father, Michael Hein, to whose memory I dedicate these illustrations.

Finally, thank you to all the amazing young people with wealth who have done this work together with us over the years. To everyone who has ever come to a workshop or a conference, ever called us up or sent us an e-mail, ever walked through our office door...without you, this book never could have existed.

Introduction

Ten percent of the people in the United States own 71 percent of the wealth.*

Now comes the point in most books about economic justice where there's a cartoon of a greedy pig in a top hat. Or the mean miserly old man, who usually looks like Mr. Burns from *The Simpsons*, stuffing his overflowing pockets with glee. It's an illustration that's meant to make us laugh and rile us up for action. The authors assume that if we are reading a book about economic justice, if we believe that this distribution of wealth is unfair, then there's no way we'd be associated with that 10 percent. It's Us against Them, plain and simple.

This is also the point in most books when we may feel totally confused. That's "we" as in young people with wealth who believe in social change. The "with wealth" part means that we're in or around that 10 percent or come from families who are. Which can make us feel like we're irrevocably condemned to be Them. The "social change" part means we believe that there is an unjust distribution of resources and that we want to be a part of working towards change. Which means we align ourselves with Us. So when the lines are laid down, if it's Us versus Them, who are We?

Is that cartoon meant to be us? Our family? Our friends? The people we love? Do we have to fight everyone in our life that falls within that wealthy 10 percent? Are we the enemy?

Based on dedicated attempts by many of us involved with Resource Generation, we can say definitively that punching ourselves in the face does not resolve any of these contradictions.

The truth is that there's a large gray area between the Us and the Them. It may be complicated in there, but, as young people with wealth who care about social change, it's our permanent address.

This doesn't mean we can't take action for social change. In fact, everything we know about having wealth can be a part of *why* we take action, can inform our awareness and commitment. We also can't forget that we have valuable resources to bring to this work—not only money, but access and connections that can be very powerful. Denying these resources helps no one.

---

* From the report, "Recent Trends in Wealth Ownership, 1983-98" by Edward N. Wolff published by the Jerome Levy Economics Institute in April 2000.

We have a chance to act *because* of who we are. Not in spite of it. And the more we understand about our experiences with wealth, the better we'll be at helping create social change, without our own private punching-party getting in the way.

"It felt like a contradiction when I was doing that work in a shelter and I had all this money and access and there were people struggling to find enough money to pay rent. It's like I was being struck in the face with the reality of how much privilege I have. Sometimes it feels like I'm going to combust. Then I understand why most people stay where they are comfortable, why people don't become activists with their wealth." —Tracy

how to use this book

First off, you should know that this book wasn't designed to be kept all neat and clean. Please feel free to write in it, spill coffee on it or toss it across the room when you think it's stupid. It's meant to be messy.

Also, this book isn't supposed to be one-size-fits-all. Just because it is written for "young people with wealth" doesn't mean we are all coming to it with the same exact experiences or the same exact goals.

This book is more like a choose-your-own-adventure. The structure is simple: the first half of the book is all about understanding privilege; the second half is about using that privilege for social change. You can take the guided tour straight through or skip around—feel free to read it backwards, sideways or upside-down. If you're stuck in a section of the book that doesn't speak to your experience, just jump ahead till you find a part that does. Hopefully at least a little of what you're looking for is somewhere in these pages.

Finally, you should know that this book isn't about telling anyone what to do. There's no Answer, no Right Way to Do It. There are tools, arguments and research tips. A bunch of quotes from other young people with wealth. Lots of comics. And a *ton* of questions.

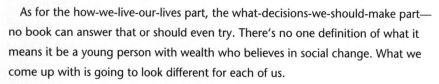

To be fair, there are also some pretty strong opinions. One is that hiding the fact we have wealth causes more harm than good. Another is that taking action with our resources is essential, and that the way we take action can be just as important as the action itself.

As for the how-we-live-our-lives part, the what-decisions-we-should-make part—no book can answer that or should even try. There's no one definition of what it means it be a young person with wealth who believes in social change. What we come up with is going to look different for each of us.

a quick note about pronouns for you grammatical sticklers...

We've chosen to bend some grammar rules and use the pronoun "they" in all occasions where otherwise writers would use "he or she." "He/she" just isn't gender neutral enough in our opinion.

CHAPTER

This Book Probably Isn't for Me

There's one main thing that everyone who calls, e-mails or walks through Resource Generation's door has in common. At one time or another they say, "I'm not sure if this is actually for me." Part of the reason why everyone is so unsure is that the heading "young people with wealth" covers a huge range of experiences. It can be hard to imagine that anyone else has gone through something even remotely similar. For example:

some people...

■ have wealth that comes from inheritance.

■ have wealth that comes from earnings.

■ share their life with someone who has wealth.

■ will inherit money later, but don't have any now.

■ grew up in a wealthy family, but will never inherit any money.

■ are part of a family foundation.

■ have wealth that comes from being famous or being a public figure.

■ have a wealthy side of the family and a not-wealthy side of the family.

■ were wealthy in another country before they came to the U.S.

■ came to the U.S. from another country without any money and made money here.

■ have had wealth come into their lives suddenly, even won the lottery.

■ have wealth that isn't sudden, but it's a relatively new thing.

■ have wealth that is generations-old.

■ inherited wealth after the death of someone close to them.

■ have wealth from a legal settlement because of an accident, a disability or a death.

■ have more wealth than their family.

■ have less wealth than their family.

■ inherited wealth without any strings attached.

■ inherited wealth with some serious strings attached.

■ had money and then lost it.

■ have money because they are from famous families.

■ have money because they are from infamous families.

■ feel like $10,000 is enormous wealth.

■ feel like $1,000,000 is enormous wealth.

■ feel like $1,000,000,000 is enormous wealth.

■ have a lot of money and don't know it yet.

■ have known they had a lot of money for a long time.

So there's definitely not one standard experience that all young people with wealth have. And there's certainly no one standard experience that all young people with wealth are looking for—which is another big reason most everyone reading this right now is thinking this book probably isn't for them.

Unfortunately, the book you hold in your hands will never be exactly like what each of us is looking for. This can be disappointing and extremely frustrating, but at least you'll know that everyone else reading is probably feeling that way too!

identity and wealth

And no, it's not just white, straight, Christian men who have wealth either, so please check all assumptions at the door. Discrimination is obviously a huge factor in the unjust distribution of resources and the reason why the majority of people who control wealth in this country aren't a very diverse bunch. For example, black families possess only 10 cents for every dollar of wealth held by white families.* However, that doesn't mean there is no diversity among young people with wealth, or that experiences with discrimination can't exist alongside experiences with wealth.

What it means to have wealth is very much defined by questions of gender, race, ethnicity, religion, ability and sexual identity. The cultural traditions and communities we are a part of are also central to shaping the ways we understand anything that happens in our lives, including having money. There really never is a room of "young people with wealth who believe in social change" where everyone has the same way of seeing or being.

a common experience of privilege

While we are definitely a diverse crowd, this book focuses on one thing we all have in common: privilege. Basically, privilege means getting an unfair special advantage because you are part of a group. Discrimination, on the other hand, means getting an unfair *dis*advantage. Having an experience of privilege in common is very different from having an experience of discrimination in common, because the two things work in completely opposite ways.

Discrimination erases individual identity. It says that everyone in the group is the same and so deserves to be treated the same, regardless of how cruel or inhumane that treatment is.

Privilege erases group identity. It says that everyone in the group is a unique and special individual, and that it's their uniqueness that entitles them to preferential treatment.

Dealing with discrimination requires reclaiming individual identity. Understanding privilege, on the other hand, requires figuring out all the ways that we're *not* unique

---

* This is an example of what's called the "racial wealth gap." This statistic comes from the book *The Hidden Cost of Being African American* (p. 47). Check out the Resource Section for more info.

individuals. We have to start looking for the unfair advantages we get just because we belong to a group, not because of anything we did on our own.

This doesn't mean we have to lose who we are. But unless we learn to see the ways privilege works in our lives, we may be helping keep the unjust distribution of resources in place without realizing it—despite our social change actions and beliefs. Despite the beauty and diversity of experience, culture and tradition in our lives. Despite who we are as individuals.

"A friend I'd known for a couple years said, 'Since your family has a lot of money now, I'm sure you must have a lot of white friends. Unless you're keeping it real.' He was assuming that wealthy people are only white people, so if you're wealthy, you're going to associate with only wealthy white people. I understood why it was easier for him to assume that a white person would be wealthy and that a black person would not be—historically, with the horrific treatment of not just African Americans but Native Americans and so many other minorities in the U.S. And when you see wealthy people in the media, more than likely it's going to be a white male. Still, the whole 'keeping it real' thing...for me to not still have my black friends—he was implying I would have sold out on everything I was before I had money."—Dawn

DECADES OF METICULOUSLY SUPPRESSED ANGER BUBBLING TO THE SURFACE, MISS MANNERS EXPLODES INTO A RAGE!!!

RUSHING TO HER BOUDOIR, SHE WORKS TIRELESSLY THROUGH THE NIGHT TO CONCOCT A MAGIC SILENCING POTION.

SHE HAS PATROLLED THE NATION EVER SINCE, MAINTAINING BLISSFUL IGNORANCE, CULTIVATING THE STATUS QUO, AND NIPPING HONEST DIALOGUE IN THE BUD.

CHAPTER

The
Classified
Files

he file is rarely left out on our desks. It's rarely even in a drawer in the living room or a cabinet in the kitchen. Instead it's down past creaky stairs, into the dark and dusty basement. Back there, behind a pile of boxes, is where we keep a thick and tattered file stamped "classified"—the place where many of us hide our experiences as young people with wealth.

Why keep this file such a secret? Some of us were told that it's rude to talk about money, or that it's dangerous for anyone to know we have wealth, or that people would treat us differently if they knew. There are a lot of variations, but the basic message always seems to be the same: wealth is something very private. It should not be discussed.

The problem is that having wealth impacts almost every part of our lives, so keeping our experiences classified takes a lot of work. Still, we give it our best shot. There's the Zip-Lip strategy: total and utter silence. And its extreme opposite, the No Biggie: masking how uncomfortable we feel by talking big whenever the subject comes up, like we don't have any feelings about it at all. There's the popular Giant Omit: editing out any parts of our life story that point to having wealth. Or its creative cousin, The Alterna-Reality: replacing those parts of our life story with invented experiences.

No matter what our strategy, this "classified" thing can make having even a simple conversation feel daunting.

Keeping our experiences with wealth classified gets in the way of more than just our conversations. It's hard to understand who we are and how we see the world when we're living undercover. The secrecy can make it tough for us to build trusting relationships. And we can't learn more about our resources because we don't talk about them with anyone or ask questions.

All of this combined makes it practically impossible for us to use our resources for social change.

EXAMPLE 1

Let's say you want to create a giving plan. How can you create a plan if you don't know how much money you have to give? How can you figure out how much money you have to give if you can't talk to an advisor or your partner or your family about your resources? How can you figure out where to give when you can't talk to anyone about being a donor?

EXAMPLE 2

Let's say you're volunteering for a housing group that's trying to get a new mixed-income housing development built. How can you tell the group that your dad plays golf with all the politicians on the local housing commission if you can't explain that he's the CEO of an important local corporation? How can you tell them he's the CEO without talking about your family's wealth? How can you tell your dad about why you're involved with the group if you can't talk about wealth with him either?

We can keep trying to cover up the details of our lives. But is it worth it? It makes it harder to understand ourselves, it takes away from our relationships, and we're certainly not going to be effective at using our resources for social change if we're busy pretending those resources aren't there.

Seems easy enough on paper. All we have to do is declassify the file and we're set. So why is this so hard?

it's hard because it's emotional

Talking about wealth is *emotional*. It can open up a whole variety pack of feelings like shame, anger, mistrust, guilt, grief and isolation. It brings up fears: fear of being taken advantage of, fear of being asked for money, fear that people will hate us. There are the totally conflicting and confusing messages that some of us get, like: "you won't ever have to worry about money" combined with "you're a spoiled brat." Or "you deserve this" combined with "you'd never be able to make it on your own." And there's the simple fact that it's heart-crushing to see other people suffer when we have more than we need. No wonder we keep this file buried down in the basement.

So here we are, a group of young people with wealth who believe in social change, who want to take action to help create a more just distribution of resources. Yet when we try to start talking about our own resources, the emotions that come up can be so overwhelming that they leave us voiceless and paralyzed.

Seems like it's about time that we come together to help each other break out of this cycle. First things first: we've got to lay all these emotions and experiences out on the table so we can take a good look at them. The more we can learn about where these feelings come from and what they're about, the better we'll be at understanding them without getting overwhelmed. The process may not be easy, but we can't let that stop us!

"These were the cards I was dealt and I need to figure out a way to make sense of it within my own life. I started to realize that the feelings of guilt—they're not very constructive. They don't really get you anywhere besides just feeling bad. So I started to look at them as my challenge to work through." — Amy

top ten ways to hide being rich

No, these really don't work. Honestly. It's kind of amazing, though, to think about how much effort and creativity we can put into keeping things classified. Sometimes there's nothing left to do but laugh at ourselves. And so, in service of the funny, here are a few popular rich-kid-in-hiding strategies.

1. **"I'll just have water."** The trick to this one is to order the cheapest thing on the menu, never get anything to drink but tap water, and spend the whole meal complaining about how expensive the place is.

2. **"I spent the weekend at my grandparents' house."** Second homes or country homes are bound to give us away. Better to pretend we were visiting relatives or family friends.

3. **"What does my mom do? Oh, she's in food service."** To hide a job title that might imply wealth, being vague helps. For example, "vice president of a huge food service corporation" just becomes "food service."

4. **"What a little spoiled brat!"** They'll never guess we're rich if we're busy making fun of other rich kids!

5. **"I'll just get out on the corner."** The only way to hide a wealthy-looking home is to never let anyone see it. This one requires *a lot* of work.

6. **"My student loan is enormous!"** There's nothing like an imaginary loan to cover up the fact that we didn't need financial aid.

7. **"Yeah, I know my shirt has a big hole, but I can't afford to get another one."** No one will know we're rich if our clothes are falling apart! The key here is to get the stuff that looks old and cheap, not artsy and vintage.

8. **"If only I had enough money for that."** As long as we constantly refer to our extremely tight budget—and complain about it—they'll never suspect otherwise.

9. **"I used the five-finger discount. Pretty cool, huh?"** Rich people would never shoplift, right? Therefore we're not rich!

10. **"I remember when I had to shovel manure."** Maybe we did have a crappy job. Maybe we were just helping out at the stable where we ride. All that matters is that it sounds like we were suffering for a paycheck, thus proving we could not possibly be rich.

quiz

Ever wonder if you're the ultimate lover? Or ponder if pink is your color? Well, this quiz won't answer that. On the other hand, it may give you a sense of what kinds of money situations raise your anxiety meter. If you notice yourself feeling uncomfortable or laughing at something you know you do, you might want to note it as something worth looking into.

1 You're listening to a speaker at a Big Justice Coalition meeting. The person next to you says, "That guy doesn't know what the hell he's talking about. He's just a trust fund baby." You say:

a. "Yeah, he can't possibly understand our struggle."

b. Nothing. Just look down at the floor and hope it will swallow you up before she figures out you're rich too.

c. Rack your brain for some way to talk more about this with her.

d. Ignore her. Whatever!

2 A friend who is having financial struggles asks for help in paying her rent this month. You:

a. Go to the ATM without any further discussion and give her twice as much as she asks for, hoping she doesn't think you're stingy.

b. Tell her you have to think about it and then avoid her. Preferably forever.

c. Have your lawyers draw up a 40-page contract describing the terms of the loan.

d. Recommend she call your friend Rita who's crazy rich.

3 The following best describes a typical conversation about money in your family:

a. What conversation?

b. Tears and bloodshed.

c. Everyone in suits at the quarterly meeting.

d. Relatively open and civil.

4 On a first date you like to:

a. Test the waters by telling stories about your "friend" who is wealthy.

b. Eat at McDonald's and complain about how Big Mac prices have gone up.

c. Bring along a pre-nup, just in case.

d. Take out your tax returns over dinner just to get it all out in the open and over with.

5 When you get a financial statement, you:

    a. Hide it under the bed and hope the dust bunnies eat it.

    b. Stare blankly and then start adding up the columns to divine the secret meaning based on numerology.

    c. Review it and then file in your super anal filing system.

    d. Shout, "I'm rich, biatch!"

6 If you need to get information about your finances, you:

    a. Aren't sure who to call.

    b. Usually know who to call for answers and advice.

    c. Know who to call, but it takes two weeks to work up to doing it.

    d. Know that Uncle Murgatroyd takes care of that stuff for you, but he gets annoyed if you ask him too many questions.

7 When a fundraiser asks you for money you feel:

    a. Like you can't say no.

    b. Like you can't say yes.

    c. Like you're not human, but just a big sack of money to them.

    d. Like hiding under the covers with a pint of Ben & Jerry's.

8 Your sweetie is trying to decide whether or not to leave a job that provides significant financial security for a job that pays less but has been a life-long dream. You say:

    a. "Do what you love, of course. Duh!"

    b. "Financial security is the prime directive, always. What's the issue here?"

    c. "Let's put our heads together and figure out all the options."

    d. "Hey, which do you think is tastier, guavas or mangos? Huh? Did you say something?"

9 You'd rather sleep on a bed of nails than talk about money with:

    a. Your friends.

    b. Anyone you're in a romantic relationship with.

    c. Anyone you work or volunteer with.

    d. Just about anybody.

10 You've been volunteering at Save the Marmots since you can remember. And every year you give $50 to be an official member of the organization. No one there knows that you could actually give a lot more than that. This year things have been particularly tight at STM and they might even have to shut down. You:

a. Decide to bite the bullet and have a talk with the person in charge of fundraising about how you can help as a donor.

b. Send a big anonymous check and then marvel with everyone else when it comes in about how lucky that was.

c. Fundraise everyone you know, including yourself.

d. Fundraise everyone you know, except yourself.

11 You know your family has a foundation because:

a. You saw it listed at the end of a PBS special and you're pretty sure that the Quincy McAllister Dooglewright Foundation refers to your grandfather.

b. Your great aunt says you can join the junior board once you have a few kids of your own and can prove you're more responsible.

c. How can you avoid it when they make the funding decisions together around your kitchen table?

d. Funny thing is, actually, you work there.

calculate your score:

There isn't a right answer to any of these quiz questions. But what fun is it if you can't calculate your score?

If you answered mostly As and Bs:
Rrrrroar! You're such a tiger! But watch out for this season's flip flop trend—you don't want everyone staring at those hammertoes.

If you answered mostly Cs:
Don't look now, but a new romance is just around the corner! All we can say is: make sure to spend a little extra time by the Lucky Charms display at your local supermarket.

If you answered mostly Ds:
Stop wasting your energy on arguing with that cantankerous co-worker. Try imagining their head as a brick of cheese and your day will be a breeze.

stereotypes of rich people

One reason many of us try to keep things classified is that we want to be seen as normal people and not some rich kid stereotype. From spoiled brats to trustafarians, snobby socialites to scrooges, American pop culture offers a whole range of images of what wealthy people are supposed to be like, and few of them are flattering. Hating rich people is practically a national pastime.

Yet at the same time *being* rich is still totally glorified. A wealthy lifestyle, with expensive status symbols from clothes to cars, is held up as the ideal, as something to aspire to. TV shows and magazines catalog the way rich people live in crazy detail. With all this envy, fascination and hatred mixed together, no wonder we worry that people won't see us for who we really are.

Things get even more complicated for those of us who are targets of racial and ethnic stereotypes about wealth. For example, stereotypes of Asians, Jews and Arabs all include versions of a greedy, money-grabbing menace. These stereotypes are more than just uncomfortable. They are used to justify discrimination and violence and to turn groups with less power into scapegoats for the unjust distribution of resources. If we start talking more openly about having wealth, are we somehow confirming these stereotypes? Are we making our communities even more of a target?

There's no easy answer here. It can help to remember, though, that these stereotypes have little to do with who we are as individuals, what our communities are like or how systems of inequality actually operate. In fact, most of these stereotypes were born out of anger at an unfair distribution of wealth—one more reason why it would especially suck to let them block us from using our resources for social change.

mirror-o-stereotypes

Unless you grew up in a bunker underground, you've probably been soaking up rich kid stereotypes for a long time. If we don't take a look at this stuff every once in a while, it can end up sneaking up on us and getting in our way. So imagine you were given some evil potion that turned you into your worst rich kid stereotype nightmare. What would you see in the mirror?

worst case scenario

Do you ever find yourself crossing your fingers, hoping maybe you could avoid that conversation about money for just a little longer—even if avoiding it is messing with your relationship?

Feeling overwhelmed by fears about what might happen can make an already tough conversation even tougher. We wish we could say that naming those fears is all it takes to get rid of them, but alas...It does make it all a little easier though.

- What's one conversation about money you've been avoiding?
- What's the worst case scenario that could happen?
- Is that worst case scenario based on a real life experience? What happened?
- Can you think of a best case scenario for the same situation? How would it go?

Family Scrapbook

Families get first dibs on teaching us about money. So taking a closer look at our family experiences can be a big help in figuring out our current relationship to wealth. Here's some space to draw or write about a few important memories.

My first memory of my family talking about money.

A recent scene of my family having a conversation about money.

A postcard from that time we did something involving giving or volunteering or philanthropy.

A diary page from a time when there was a family conflict about money.

role plays are fun

Everybody loves role plays. Okay, well maybe not everybody. *Some* people do. And lucky for you, you're reading a book and not stuck in a workshop, so participation is optional.

This role play is useful for practicing a conversation you're feeling nervous about. As you might imagine, you need a friend to play along.

1. Think about a conversation you have had or are planning to have with someone in your life about your resources.

2. Write down some questions you would like to include in the conversation or wish you had included in the past.

3. Explain the whole scenario to your role-playing buddy. Make sure to show them those questions you wrote down too.

4. Here's the tricky part: your role play buddy is going to play *you*. You are going to play the other person. The idea is to get a glimpse of what it would be like to be on the other side of the conversation.

what if someone asks me for money?

Many of us dread being asked for money, and this fear can keep us from being more open about our wealth. Sometimes it helps to remember that asking someone for money can be even more terrifying than being asked. So it's generally a stressful situation for all involved.

It's a lot less scary, though, if we can get used to saying both yes and no. It also helps to have a clearer picture of how much we can give and what our criteria is for making decisions. There's a ton of info on developing a giving process coming up in Chapter 11, and Chapter 12 can help you figure out how much to give. In the meantime, these questions are helpful for looking at the way being asked for money makes you feel.

- Have you ever had to ask anyone for money? What was it like?

- Have you ever had anyone ask you for money? What was it like?

- Have you ever said yes to a request? Have you ever said no? How did it go?

- Which is easier for you in general, saying yes or saying no? How come?

- How important is the way someone asks? How come?

- Are you more or less comfortable with the situation depending on who is asking? Or on what they are asking for?

- Do you feel there are valid and invalid reasons for someone to ask for your help? How do you decide which is which?

- What kinds of things do you worry about? That your relationship will change? That you'll be taken advantage of? That the money won't be used well? That it will just lead to more requests?

- What could be some positive outcomes of being asked for money?

so what do you do?

Having wealth can mean having more options about work and school than most people have. While the upside to this is obvious, there can also be a downside. More options can be overwhelming. There's a pressure to get it right. There's the confusing weirdness of getting paid when you don't need to get paid. Or the confusing weirdness of *not* getting paid when you don't need to get paid. And trying to avoid situations where someone asks, "So what do you do?" means avoiding all cocktail parties—which is no good, since everyone needs a cocktail sometimes.

There's no right way to figure this out. But it can definitely help to step back and gain some clarity.

■ When you were little, what did you say you wanted to be when you grew up?

■ How would you answer that question now?

■ How do you feel about what you're doing now?

■ How do you support yourself financially? How do you feel about this?

■ How did your family talk about work when you were growing up? What kind of messages did you get? What messages did you get about the purpose of school and education?

■ Have you ever had a job where you got paid, but you didn't need the money? Or a job where you didn't get paid because you didn't need the money? How did you feel about it?

■ How does what you're paid—or not paid—affect the way you view the value of your work?

■ How does it affect the way you talk about your work with others?

■ If you could wave a magic wand and create your ideal work or school situation, what would it be?

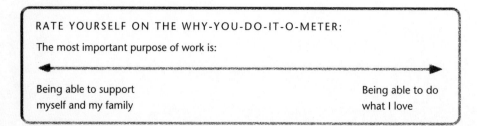

RATE YOURSELF ON THE WHY-YOU-DO-IT-O-METER:

The most important purpose of work is:

◄─────────────────────────────────────►

Being able to support
myself and my family

Being able to do
what I love

social change star

Imagine you're being interviewed by Barbara Walters. Except instead of asking about that affair with Angelina Jolie, she wants to know more about your belief in social change...

■ Tell me about someone whose activism has inspired you.

■ What is your first memory of something that wasn't fair or just?

■ What is your first memory of having more than someone else? Having less than someone else?

■ Tell me about an issue or movement you are passionately involved in. What inspired you to get involved?

■ What's something going on right now that you want to learn more about or get more involved in?

■ How would you describe your vision of social change?

■ How has having wealth influenced that vision of change?

■ Do you think there are ways that having wealth has made it easier for you to get involved in social change? More difficult?

LUCY

I HAD SEEN SEUNG AROUND SCHOOL BEFORE, BUT AFTER I SAW HER IN THAT SKINNY TIE, I DECIDED TO EMPLOY OPERATION: SHAMELESS WOOING.

CAMPUS MAIL · OFF CAMPUS MAIL

i think you're cute. call x5689

WE PLAYED THE GETTING-TO-KNOW-YOU GAME.

SO, WHERE ARE YOU FROM?

NEW YORK CITY.

OH YEAH? WHAT PART?

UPTOWN.

Ah, college... CLEAN-SLATE CITY. BECAUSE THERE ARE A LOT OF THINGS YOU CAN'T TELL ABOUT SOMEONE WHEN YOU LIVE IN IDENTICAL ROOMS WITH IDENTICAL FURNITURE, EAT IDENTICAL CAFETERIA FOOD AND DO THE SAME THINGS ALL DAY.

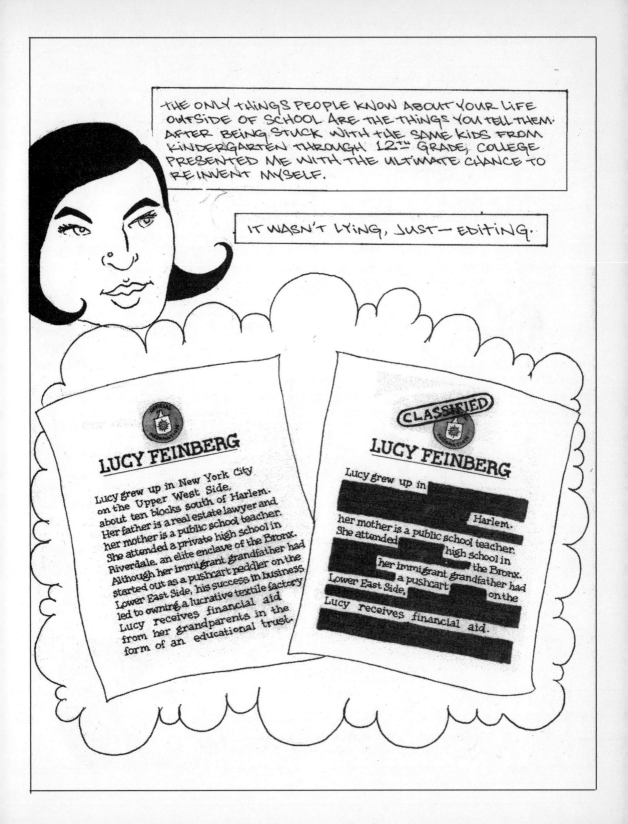

CHAPTER

Wealth=
Class
Privilege

What does it mean to be a young person with wealth anyway? If we went by some of the sitcoms and soap operas we grew up with, it'd be pretty easy to define: a secret stash of cash in the wall safe, champagne parties, private planes, a butler with a British accent. That definition also makes it easy for most of us to say, "Sure, we have more than we need, but it's not like we're *rich*." Of course some people do go to fancy parties all night, shop all day and generally live it up like an episode of *Lifestyles of the Rich and Famous*. But what *really* defines the lifestyles of the young and wealthy?

what it really looks like...

Having wealth as a young person means we've got tons of choices about everything from where we live to what kind of work we do. It's about the freedom to make plans for the future based on our dreams, and being able to take risks because we have resources to fall back on if we fail.

Wealth doesn't protect us from disappointment and loss, but it does make all the difference in how we live through those hard times. It changes the way we get treated in a hospital or a courtroom. It can allow us the time to mourn without worrying about our family's financial status. Having wealth is a safety net, a backup plan and an expanded set of options all rolled into one.

For those of us who grew up wealthy, wealth means things like afterschool lessons and tutors, summer camps and vacations. It means we had access to career-building opportunities through family friends or family businesses and foundations. It means we were told, "You can be whatever you want to be" by everyone, especially our teachers—and we knew our family could afford the education we'd need to make good on that. And if wealth is a relatively new thing in our lives, it means having the option to give the next generation a similar set of opportunities.

Having wealth is about the big stuff like not having debt or car payments. And the small stuff like catching a cultural reference. It's about knowing how to talk and dress and act to make the bigwigs comfortable (even if we wear ripped fishnets and give them the finger instead). It's about having access to those bigwigs in the first place.

All this adds up to something much more than bank accounts or luxuries. Money alone can't define what it means to be a young person with wealth. The word that describes all this stuff is *class privilege.**

class privilege is a mediator

Right about now you may be thinking, "But all the class privilege in the world doesn't erase discrimination." Class privilege is useless against the everyday racism that people of color have to deal with. It doesn't stop sexism or homophobia. It's no shield against oppression at all.

---

* Wait a second, this book never defined class! Or classism! It's only talking about class privilege, and only defining it by example! Bad book! The thing is, this book's focus is on understanding privilege through personal experience. (Check out the preface for the whole philosophy behind doing it this way.) Understanding privilege is only a first step towards understanding class and classism, but it's still a pretty crucial one. As for next steps, the Resource Section has a list of books that lay out much more in-depth analyses of class and classism.

But while class privilege does not insulate, it can negotiate—it can serve as a mediator for those of us who have to deal with discrimination. It gives us access to concrete services like good doctors and lawyers. It can mean having enough resources, mobility and connections to escape a painful or dangerous situation instead of being trapped there. It also grants us more abstract necessities like being able to take the time and space to heal from traumatic experiences. Class privilege gives us options that other people struggling against the same forces just don't have.*

class privilege is an amplifier

Class privilege can also come as a package deal with many other kinds of privilege, like white privilege or male privilege. In this case, class privilege acts as an amplifier. It can turn the noise up so loud that it's hard to hear anything else but our own experiences—leaving us a little bit hard of hearing, and making it even tougher to sort out what's going on.

This doesn't mean that understanding privilege is some competition and the person with the least privilege wins the most social change points. It just means that the more privilege we have, the more challenging the process of understanding it can be. Having more privilege usually puts us ahead of the game in most situations. In this case, ironically, it means we're gonna have to work harder.

---

* bell hooks lays this idea out in *Where We Stand: Class Matters*. Check out the chapter "Class and Race: The New Black Elite."

"My mom and dad divorced when I was young. With my mom, we got a lot of assistance on clothes, utility bills, heating bills, stuff like that. We got a monthly food basket.

But with my dad, at that time I would say he was in the top five percent economically and drove luxury sports sedans and went on international vacations whenever he wanted to and was able to buy us what we needed. It was weird, because it was always a very rigid line between my lifestyle with my dad and my lifestyle with my mom to the point that I even had two totally different wardrobes.

It was a very nasty situation in my teen years. I realized that I had access to certain things with my dad that I didn't have with my mom. I eventually made the decision to leave my mom and stay with my dad. But I think that there's always been some guilt there at the same time.

When I open my mouth people are much more willing to listen to me. I have the advantage, in the end, of being a white male. I'm a straight white male, a Christian straight white male. It is more difficult for me to see the oppression that other people face. There have been dozens of times in my life where I just literally shrugged off oppression, not realizing what it was. I've never been able to understand how I managed to forget about a lot of the class discrimination I experienced living with my mom. Not just manage to forget but lose the tools to discern."
—Garrett

"ANJALI"

AS WOMEN OF COLOR, OBVIOUSLY THE LATEST BUDGET CUTS ARE HITTING US THE HARDEST. NONE OF US CAN AFFORD TO TAKE ANOTHER HIT!

I WONDER WHAT THEY MAKE OF ME— THEY MUST ASSUME I'M IN THE SAME BOAT AS THEM. WHAT IF THEY KNEW I DON'T EVEN NEED FINANCIAL AID?

...OR MAYBE THEY TOTALLY KNEW. MAYBE THEY WERE LIKE, "WHAT IS SHE DOING HERE? LISTEN TO HOW SHE TALKS— SHE SOUNDS LIKE SHE'S TRYING TO BE WHITE. SHE THINKS SHE'S BETTER THAN US..."

THERE'S STUFF I CAN REALLY IDENTIFY WITH HERE IN THIS GROUP — BUT HOW AM I SUPPOSED TO BE UP FRONT ABOUT WHERE I'M COMING FROM?

DO I

CHAPTER  4

Class
Privilege →
Wealth

The weird thing about class privilege is that a person can have a lot of it without having any money in the bank. Those of us who grew up in wealthy families have some experience with this. We may be inheriting money later in life, but have no access to it now. Our family may have used most of its wealth to create a foundation instead of passing it on to the kids. Some of us have been cut off financially because of our politics, our sexuality, our religion, our gender identity, our choice of partner or our lifestyle. Yet even if we have zero dollars to our name, we still inherit class privilege—and that can have a big impact on our lives. We can literally be "young people with wealth" *without* wealth.*

How is this possible? It makes more sense if we check out a whole other side of class privilege. In the last chapter we looked at how having class privilege defines the experience of having wealth. But class privilege also *creates* wealth.

For example, think about what it's like to go to a job interview. Sure, much of whether or not we get the job is based on our own individual fabulousness. Still, class privilege has a pretty big hand in how we get seen...

---

* A quick note about vocab: having money is *part* of having class privilege, but you can still have class privilege without having money. From this point on, the book uses the words class privilege and wealth pretty much interchangeably. Both terms are meant to include experiences of having privilege *with* money as well as experiences of having privilege *without* money.

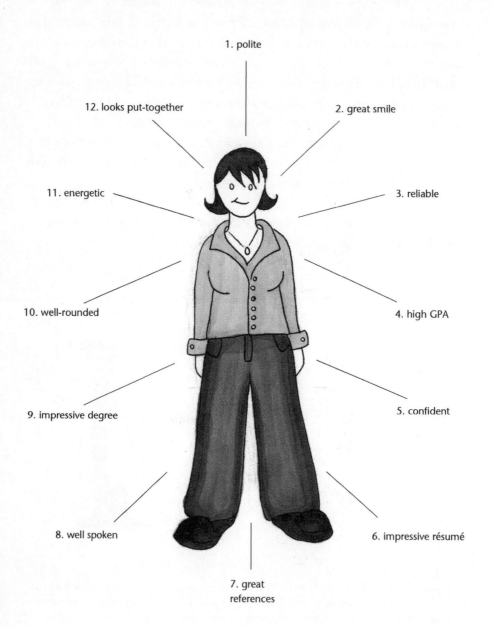

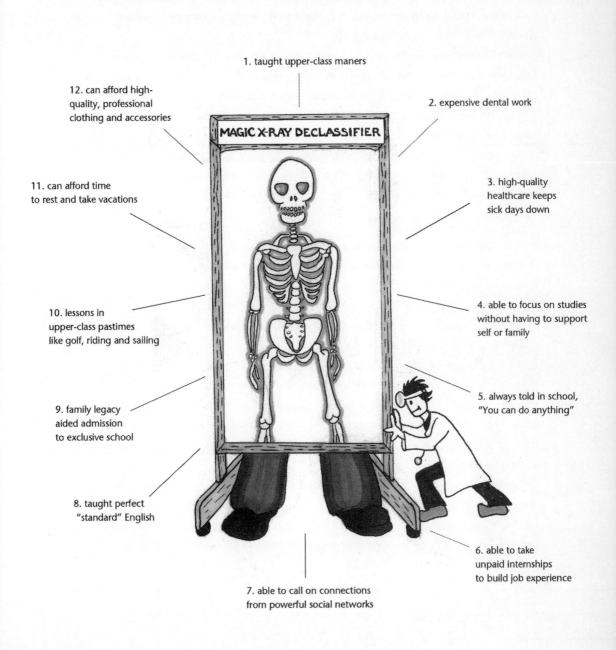

class privilege affects our financial future

A job interview is only one of many situations where class privilege affects our financial future. Every time we walk into a bank for a loan, into a real estate broker's office for a home, even into an important meeting at work, being a young person with wealth gives us an unspoken advantage.

Another advantage comes from the fact that class privilege can place us in some very powerful networks. Networks are one of the main ways people find out about things like jobs, housing and business opportunities. Class privilege gives us access to exclusive formal associations like alumni groups and prestigious clubs, as well as informal webs of influential neighbors, family and friends.

These connections don't just tell us about possible opportunities, they can also help us act on them. When someone "in the know" puts in a good word for us, it transforms us from an anonymous name into a friendly face—and that can often make all the difference.

this doesn't mean we don't work hard

Thinking about the impact of class privilege on our lives can be unsettling, especially if we grew up wealthy and don't have any other class experience to compare it to. We want to say that our successes happen because we deserve them—because we worked hard, because we studied and sacrificed, because we were committed to our goals. We want to say that maybe we had that privilege, but we chose not to use it, that we didn't need it, that we could make it on our own merits.

The problem is that privilege isn't something that can be turned on or off. While money can be laid aside unused, privilege is deeply embedded in our lives. It's a part of the experiences that make us who we are, that shape how we see the world and the way the world sees us. Class privilege even becomes a part of our bodies, from straight teeth to a "firm" handshake.

Acknowledging how class privilege impacts our lives doesn't have to mean abandoning pride in ourselves. Our hard work is still hard work. Our fabulousness is still fabulous. It just means that, as young people with wealth, the story of where we are and how we got there is more complicated than a list of our merits. There's a lot more there to uncover.

word finds are fun

Don't forget to check for diagonals and backwards words!

```
E  S  O  Y  P  M  A  C  R  E  M  M  U  S  Y  E
N  L  P  I  A  N  O  L  E  S  S  O  N  S  P  R
V  O  F  O  U  N  D  A  T  I  O  N  R  O  A  T
E  O  V  A  C  A  T  I  O  N  S  R  H  H  R  R
S  H  Y  C  D  M  O  N  C  I  C  U  M  U  E  P
E  C  C  N  O  N  L  I  L  R  A  O  R  A  H  A
C  S  A  O  O  U  U  P  N  U  T  U  E  I  T  U
O  E  G  R  O  D  N  F  E  E  C  S  B  E  S  S
N  T  E  O  R  E  E  T  T  U  T  O  R  M  Y
D  A  L  T  D  T  T  B  R  S  E  E  C  O  E  E
H  V  C  E  Y  B  R  E  T  Y  U  C  O  P  U  O
O  I  D  N  B  R  A  C  E  S  C  R  T  T  A  I
M  R  A  C  T  E  N  B  N  S  N  L  T  O  O  C
E  P  C  R  E  D  I  T  D  W  N  P  U  C  E  O
O  R  C  N  S  U  A  S  O  C  O  F  I  B  F  I
R  P  C  T  E  O  C  O  E  C  N  S  U  R  S  S
```

word list:

Tutor	Credit	Therapy
Trust Fund	Vacations	Braces
Legacy	Private School	No Debt
Country Club	Piano Lessons	Summer Camp
Own Room	Second Home	Foundation

47

deep thoughts about class privilege

Here are some seriously heavy questions about the impact of class privilege in our lives. Woo hoo! Yeah!

Okay, maybe that's a little overzealous. It'd probably be much more fun to watch *MacGyver* reruns and eat Funyuns. But even though it isn't easy, understanding our privilege has the potential to change our lives and our relationships in some amazing ways. Plus, the more we understand, the better we'll be at using our privilege for social change.

A few of the questions here are based specifically on stuff in Chapters 3 and 4, so you might want to check them out if you haven't already, just to get the most out of this exercise. And, obviously, depending on your background and what's up for you right now in your life, some of these questions will be more or less relevant. Feel free to skip anything that doesn't pertain...

big decisions

■ Think about a big decision you've made recently. Were there ways that having class privilege factored into that decision?

■ Has having class privilege ever affected the way you've been able to cope with a difficult or painful time in your life? How so?

■ What's one of the biggest risks you've taken—or wish you could have taken— in your life? Were there resources of your own or family resources that you could have fallen back on if it didn't work out? Did that affect your choice to take the risk?

work and school

■ Has having class privilege affected your education? How so? Has it had an affect on your choices about schools? About what to study?

■ Has having class privilege had an affect on your decisions about work? Has it had an impact on your salary, income or level of prestige associated with your work?

where you live

■ Has having class privilege played a role in your housing decisions? Has it affected where you've lived in the past? Where you live now? The way other people involved, like brokers, realtors and landlords, treated you? Whether you rent or own? If you own, did it impact the way you paid for your home?

48

discrimination

- Are there ways that class privilege *hasn't* made any difference for you in dealing with discrimination? How so?

- Are there ways that class privilege *has* made a difference for you in dealing with discrimination? How so?

- How have your experiences with discrimination impacted the way you understand class privilege?

other kinds of privilege

- Do you have other kinds of privilege in addition to class privilege? How does that affect the way you look at your experiences with class privilege?

- Has there ever been a time when having privilege made it harder to hear what someone was trying to say to you?

If you grew up with wealth...

- Were there ways that class privilege had an impact on your daily life? How so?

- Did having class privilege ever affect the way people treated you? How?

- Did having class privilege affect the way you saw your own potential and your role is in the world? How?

If wealth is a more recent thing in your life...

- Are there ways that having class privilege has changed your daily life?

- Are there ways that having class privilege has changed the way people treat you?

- Has having class privilege affected your sense of what's possible in your life and your hopes for the future? How so?

social situations

- Have you ever been in a situation where you knew the "right" way to act because of your class privilege? Or the "right" way to speak? Or where you got a joke or a reference to something that you understood because you had class privilege?

financial status

- Does having class privilege affect your current income and expenses? Do you have loans? Car payments? Mortgage payments? Do you have a financial safety net or family resources you can fall back on?

- Does having class privilege affect the way you are treated at the bank? How?

health

- Does having class privilege impact the kind of healthcare you receive? The quality of your doctors? Dental work? Therapy?

- If you've had to deal with a major illness or injury, either your own or a family member's, did having class privilege have an impact on your choices about treatments and options?

legal system

- If you've had to deal with the police or the legal system, did having class privilege affect your options and the outcome of the experience? How?

"In boarding school, I remember being told, 'You guys are the cream of the cream. The education you are receiving here is preparing you to be leaders in the world.' I realized that the other young people in my class weren't necessarily that special. They were nice, but they weren't so great. It just made me wonder why these people get to be the leaders. Why do I get to be the leader? There's no real reason for that. It's the luck of the draw."
—Christian

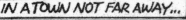
IN A TOWN NOT FAR AWAY...

CHAPTER  5

The Fancyhood

If understanding class privilege were a giant onion, then so far we've only looked at one layer of it: our individual experiences. If we want to see more about how the whole big, smelly thing works, we need to peel off another layer. We need to look at how class privilege plays out in *institutions*.

who are the institutions in your neighborhood?

What are institutions? Some quick examples: governments, schools, hospitals, churches and banks. Institutions shape the way a society runs, impacting people's lives both day-to-day and long-term. They are organizations that lay down rules and rights, distribute resources and information, and stamp what's legit and what isn't. Institutions have a force that's all their own—their agendas and influence hold a greater collective power than that of any of the individuals who run them.

Sometimes it's easiest to see how institutions affect our lives by looking at them at a neighborhood level.* The average wealthy neighborhood is chock full of examples...

---

* The inspiration for this section comes from the "Undoing Racism" training created by the People's Institute for Survival and Beyond.

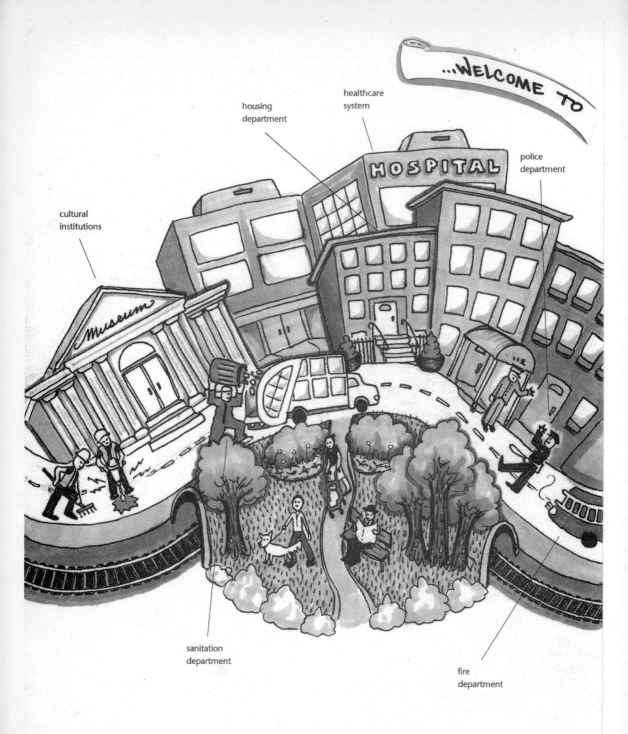

THE FANCYHOOD...

food
distribution

school
system

public works
department

SCHOOL

ENTIRE FOODS

STOP

FIRE

PARK-N-RIDE

transportation
department

parks and recreation
department

class privilege in policies and legislation

So how does class privilege show up on an institutional level? For starters, it makes a pretty blatant appearance in some policies and legislation. One example is the "legacy policy" that most private colleges and many public colleges have in their admissions departments. A legacy policy basically says that if you have relatives that are alumni, your application will be granted special consideration. Legacy students make up between 10 to 15 percent of the freshman class at most Ivy League universities. At Harvard, 40 percent of the children of alumni are admitted versus 11 percent of regular applicants.* The legacy policy means that a family tradition of attendance at an elite university helps guarantee admissions for the next generation.

Institutional class privilege is also written right into the federal tax code. One good example of this is a tax deduction for homeowners called the mortgage interest deduction. This deduction is supposed to help people buy their own homes. However, the larger your mortgage and the higher your tax bracket, the more you benefit from it. The result is that the federal government actually ends up subsidizing wealthy people's purchases of bigger, fancier homes.

Legacy policies and tax credits are just two of the more obvious examples of how class privilege plays out at an institutional level. But there's also a more subtle kind of institutional preference shown to people with wealth that marks our lives.

class privilege means
institutions treat us differently

In fact, when everybody at RG started coming up with examples of ways they've seen people with wealth get preferential treatment from institutions, we ended up with a mega-list. It was kind of boring to write out that way, so instead we made up a fake newspaper based on the examples (and one of our favorite TV shows about rich kids). Welcome to the *Class Privilege Times*—all the news that's never in print!

---

* These statistics come from the article "Meritocracy in Universities," in the January 8th, 2004 issue of the *Economist*.

The Class Privilege Times

Dangerous Dump in 90210? No Way!

We can finally stop worrying about whether or not our 90210 zip code will host a major toxic waste containment facility. Commented the mayor, "Perhaps the greatest influence on my decision was the fact that I live in 90210 too. So you can bet I didn't want those toxic fumes next door! Besides, while ToxiCorp has tried to demonstrate that they will bring more jobs to our area and help contribute to the community, we don't need their help. There was just no reason for us to agree to the facility." A ToxiCorp representative stated that they were now exploring areas where property values were "more of a bargain."

Local Teen Sentenced Today

Kelly Taylor was arraigned today on charges of possessing a small amount of cocaine. She received a sentence of probation and counseling. A courthouse commentator noted, "Kelly was particularly lucky in her sentencing because not only is she white and able to afford a good lawyer—paving the way for a markedly easier experience with the criminal justice system—she could also afford more expensive powdered cocaine instead of its cheaper cousin, crack cocaine. If she'd been caught carrying the same amount of crack she would have had a mandatory five year prison term!"

Benefactors Keeping Quality of Life High

While budget cuts have meant fewer services and a lower quality of life for most of the surrounding areas, the quality of life here in 90210 continues to soar. Thanks to donations from local benefactors like Rush Sanders and the Martin Family Foundation, in just the last eight months improvements have been made to our local library, community center and opera house. Says Rush Sanders, "We can't rely on government spending to ensure that 90210 is a great place to live. We've got to take care of our own community—and luckily we've got the deep pockets to do it well!"

Police Treat Local Residents with Courtesy

Police responded promptly to a call when a break-in at Casa Walsh was reported last night. Cindy Walsh stated that the officers were very polite, even wiping their feet on the doormat before entering, and that they did their best to expedite the whole process. Said daughter Brenda Walsh, "I feel confident the officers will do everything they can to find the burglar and keep us safe."

Relationship with Bank Paves Way For Mortgage

When David Silver went to Beverly Hills Bank for a mortgage on his first home, it was smooth sailing. Says his loan officer, "We've done business with David's family for some time now, so I was comfortable signing off on this loan." In addition to getting quick approval and a good rate, David's mortgage payments will be even lower because his father co-signed and chipped in with a

large down payment. His loan officer also mentioned that, "Although redlining [the practice of refusing to insure loans in minority areas] is illegal, we do find that everything just runs smoother when loaning to a white person moving into a white neighborhood. Especially a wealthy white person moving into a wealthy white neighborhood!"

Local Services Running Like Clockwork

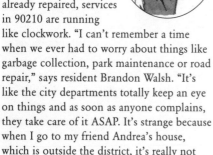

With the recent pothole on Alta Dena Drive already repaired, services in 90210 are running like clockwork. "I can't remember a time when we ever had to worry about things like garbage collection, park maintenance or road repair," says resident Brandon Walsh. "It's like the city departments totally keep an eye on things and as soon as anyone complains, they take care of it ASAP. It's strange because when I go to my friend Andrea's house, which is outside the district, it's really not the same. A lot of times there's uncollected trash and the traffic light on her street is always broken."

Excellent Insurance Makes All the Difference in Grandparent's Hospitalization

We spoke today with Donna Martin about her beloved grandmother's recent hospitalization. "The fact that we could afford such great health insurance for her made a huge difference," said Martin. "She really needs this heart operation and we didn't have to go through tons of red tape or arguing with an HMO to get permission for it." Martin also pointed out that the family arranged for a private room and a private nurse. Commented Martin, "Since even the best hospitals can get pretty busy, we wanted to make sure she had her privacy and was always being attended to."

Realtors Tell African American Couple No Homes Available Here

Despite being qualified buyers, a wealthy African American couple hoping to move into 90210 was told by a number of local realtors that there were no homes available. However, our news team has discovered that both the Arnolds and the Keates recently put their homes on the market.

One realtor explained that she avoided showing the couple these homes because she believed keeping the neighborhood "as white as possible" would protect property values. She also mentioned a recent security patrol "snafu" as "proof" that a more integrated neighborhood "just causes problems." As reported previously by this paper, the boyfriend of Charise Ashe [daughter of 90210's only African American family] was mistakenly harassed and beaten by a security patrol while attempting to bring her flowers.

Improvements at West Beverly Hills High

Local public school West Beverly Hills High has announced some exciting improvements for this fall. Vice Principal Yvonne Teasley says, "Look for smaller class sizes as well as some great new teachers. And a brand new computer room!" Even with this year's state budget cuts in school funding, West Beverly High isn't feeling the pinch because this wealthy district's substantial local property taxes more than cover school budget needs.

invisibility

Fake newspapers aside, when we look at the actual media we rarely see a connection made between why some people don't have enough and why other people are getting preferential treatment. No one asks questions like, "Why do rich kids have higher graduation rates?" Instead, they only look at dropout rates. No one talks about how, when institutions are under-funded and languishing, people with wealth often choose to opt out of the system entirely and pay for private services like schools, security and healthcare. It's as if this whole realm of privilege were somehow invisible.

Yet as young people with wealth, we see with our own eyes the institutional advantages class privilege brings. We experience the benefit of them every day.

what it looks like

Because institutions are created and led mainly by people with class privilege, our own privilege gives us the inside scoop on how to act and speak when we walk in the front door. We know how to ask for what we need and how to make sure we get it. All the signs of our privilege, especially the ones that are a part of our bodies, signal to those in charge that they should treat us with respect instead of suspicion. Sometimes the class privilege networks we're a part of even personally connect us to the people running the place.

The more privilege we have, the more institutions are designed with us in mind, making complicated forms and procedures feel almost intuitive. Having class privilege doesn't mean we never have bad, frustrating or abusive experiences with institutions. It does mean our complaints are taken seriously, and that we're more likely to succeed in getting them addressed.

the more we have, the more we get

Our institutional advantage and access affects every part of our lives. It impacts our health and well-being. It helps us obtain necessities like safe housing, good healthcare and quality education, and enables us to act on our dreams. It grants us what every person needs to both survive and thrive.

Yet while every person needs these things, most people aren't getting them. Since institutions center on serving those with privilege, resources aren't distributed based on need. Instead, the more we have, the more we get.

If we're committed as young people with wealth to a more just distribution of resources, we need to seriously commit to changing the way institutions work.

write for the Class Privilege Times

You know you always wanted to be a reporter. Create a dramatic photograph or incisive exposé about one way you've seen class privilege play out in institutions.

"People in power tend to pass on their power to people like them. If powerful people are identifying with you more easily, or with your community more easily, they put more funding into your community, or they hire people who look like them, or they look more favorably towards schools that have students like them. Chances are the power is going to pass into really similar hands. I think I'd be naive to say that, oh, well, my family was totally immune to all that. It would be nice to be able to say that, but it's probably not true."—Ariana

CHAPTER

The Not So Level Playing Field

Since we just spent the last three chapters looking at how class privilege gives us a huge advantage, it would be pretty strange for us to turn around and say that everyone in the United States has an equal shot at becoming wealthy. Yet the prevailing belief right now in this country is exactly that. It often gets referred to as the "level playing field." According to this idea, becoming rich has nothing to do with luck or privilege—it's solely a factor of merit and hard work. Therefore, everyone has a fair chance: as long as you're smart enough, as long as you're willing to sweat for it, you'll become rich, even if you started with nothing.

A quick illustration of how deep this belief runs: in a 2000 *Time* magazine poll, about 40 percent of those polled said that they expected to be or already were part of the wealthiest *one percent* of Americans.*

On the other hand, according to our experiences as young people with wealth, the "level playing field" looks a lot more like this:

the level playing field idea leads to some big problems

Here's the problem with the level playing field idea: it implies that the only reason someone *isn't* wealthy is that they aren't working hard enough or that they aren't smart enough.

So according to the level playing field theory, everyone may not have an equal share, but they have what they deserve because they sweated for it fair and square.

Institutions have no affect on the way resources are distributed, so it doesn't make much difference if they show preference to the privileged. In fact, since privilege has

---

* This poll comes from the article "Two Men, Two Visions" in the November 6, 2000 issue of
  Time magazine.

nothing to do with the creation of wealth, there's no reason to take it into consideration at all.

It's only when we can show how the playing field is severely slanted in favor of those with privilege that talking about institutional change and a more just distribution of resources starts to make sense.

we can help paint a more realistic picture

This is why there's a real role for us here as young people with wealth who believe in social change. People have been speaking out about the unjust distribution of resources and the uneven playing field in the U.S. for about as long as this country has been around. But even the most radical rich people rarely back them up by putting their own experiences with privilege out there. It's time for us to step up and start talking about our first-hand experiences with the ways that class privilege determines wealth.

"There's this idea that everybody here can make something of themselves. You just have to work hard and you'll do well. That has a corollary, which is if you're not doing well, you're what's wrong. I think that there's that blaming the victim kind of thing. It leads to a lot of assumptions that if you are wealthy you're doing something right."—Sarah

CHAPTER

Money
Stories

Shared stories bring people together. They tell us something about who we are and how we are connected, about how we see ourselves and the world we live in. Like the tale of the craaaaaazy spring break that unites the girls of Delta Delta Delta. Or that story about Grandpa Al and the goat that the family always tells.

For those of us who have inherited wealth, there's bound to be a story about where the money came from. If wealth is a relatively recent thing in our lives, we've probably already begun shaping a new story about where that money came from. Either way, it's worth taking a closer look at these narratives because they can play a big role in how we understand our own privilege and how we talk about it with others.

haven't I heard that one before?

At "Making Money Make Change," an annual retreat that RG helps put on for young people with wealth, there's always one particularly intense part of the weekend. It's when everyone attending, usually around 60 people or so, sits in a big circle and each person has a few minutes to tell the story of where their money comes from.

While some tales of sudden wealth center on chance, the majority of the money stories begin to take on a strange similarity to each other. They focus on one person, often a man, and they center on how his hard work, intelligence, ingenuity, willingness to take risks and temerity lead to eventual financial good fortune. While the details of each story vary, the same plotlines—even the same phrases—occur again and again: "pulled himself up by the bootstraps," "wise investor," "rags to riches," "worked day and night," "never took a handout" and "self-made man."

what's the story behind all these stories?

How do so many of us end up with such similar stories? It has a lot to do with that national belief in the level playing field (see Chapter 6) and the idea that wealth is earned through hard work and merit alone. Shared stories are often more about validating big beliefs like this than about what actually went down.* That's why, even though we're all coming from such different experiences, our tales end up sounding the same.

---

* Eduardo Bonilla-Silva's book *Racism Without Racists* was a big influence on this chapter. Check out the chapter "Color-Blind Racism's Racial Stories," where he looks at the connection between stories white people tell about race and what keeps racism in place.

This isn't to say these money stories are lies. People did and do work their asses off. They are smart, industrious, brave and committed to taking care of their families. But aren't there other factors? Other people involved? Does anyone ever really do it all on their own? By retelling these stories are we justifying ideas—like the level playing field—that we don't even believe in?

The usual story:

I started out with nothing. My father worked in a factory and didn't even graduate high school— so you could say I really am a self-made man. I risked everything to open my first grocery store, and things were so hard that at first I wasn't sure we'd make it through. But I worked day and night, night and day, and it turned out I had a real knack for the grocery business. Now I own a chain of 10 successful supermarkets.

What gets left out:

His wife who took care of their home and their children.

His in-laws who lent him their small savings to help him start the first store.

The hundreds of thousands of people around the world who grew, processed and transported the things that were sold in the supermarkets.

His local friends who went out of their way to shop at the first store and encouraged others to do so.

A number of tax cuts for those in the higher tax brackets in the 1980s that allowed him to increase his savings.

The bank that gave him his first loan, in part because his store was in a white neighborhood and so considered a more acceptable risk.

The team of financial advisors that grew his profits through investments and helped him find tax shelters so that he could keep more of the money he earned.

All the workers, from cashiers to managers to janitors, whose wages were held low enough to keep profits high.

Grocer lobby groups who pushed for cost-cutting policies on food production, agriculture, transportation and labor.

so much that gets left out

Most money stories leave out all kinds of important factors. For one, a lot of people already had some kind of privilege in their favor, like male privilege or white privilege or heterosexual privilege, even if they didn't have class privilege. Often at least one person, if not a whole family's worth of people, was helping back the story's hero up, taking care of them, feeding and cleaning and caring for children and giving them the freedom to "work night and day." It takes a lot of people to build a building or keep a company running or create a product, not just the person in charge who's reaping most of the profits. And it usually takes a lot of people working at lower wages to keep that profit high. Then there are all the institutional laws and policies that can make the difference between success and failure: tax cuts and subsidies, policies and legislation, connections with banks and investors, labor relations and wages.

There are also tons of factors that play into how someone becomes wealthy through investing besides just the wisdom of their investment—what about all the workers, companies, policies and even governments behind those profitable returns?

it takes a village...

It takes a whole lot of people and institutions all working together to create just one person's wealth.* This means that if we want to rewrite our money stories to tell the full tale, they're going to be longer, messier and more complicated. They'll need to examine questions of privilege, history and luck, not just one individual's dedication.

Rewriting our money stories doesn't mean we have to edit out the celebration of hard work and ingenuity. That's still a part of the plot. Instead it means inking in the other factors that allow one hard worker to become wealthy while another hard worker struggles on. Telling a new kind of money story can go a long way toward challenging the national belief in the level playing field and underscoring why we need institutional change. It's one way we can stop justifying the unequal distribution of resources and start helping to challenge it.

---

* United for a Fair Economy and Responsible Wealth lay this argument out in, "I Didn't Do It Alone: Society's Contribution to Individual Wealth and Success," a report by Chuck Collins, Scott Klinger and Mike Lapham. It's full of interviews with successful entrepreneurs breaking down the whole "self-made" myth. Check it out at www.faireconomy.org/notalone/.

THE MATRIX REINVESTED

"My parents came from working and middle class families. My dad became a professor of finance and over the course of my life he's steadily been making more money. By the time I was in college my parents had made money on investments and started a business selling study guides for people taking the Chartered Financial Analyst exam. When I was 26 my folks sold the business for many millions of dollars.

There's different ways to look at how they made this money. One is to look at how it had to do with the skin privilege my parents had—I mean my dad's family is Irish and German and my mom's family is Russian Jewish. So the way whiteness has worked and how they've been allowed to be white is part of why my parents had access to a greater range of opportunities.

Another way to look at it is they were really hard-working and they set out to make a lot of money. I have a lot of respect for the work that they did and the way they went from working their way through college to being multi-millionaires.

Then there's another analysis that asks, what were they actually doing? Investing. My dad's analysis about investing is, 'that's the way the free market works.' But there's also the idea that you're loaning money to companies that are raping the earth, destroying people's homelands and paying money to special interest lobby groups that destroy democracy even in our own country.

I feel like what my parents valued was financial security because they wanted to take care of their family, and I don't think that's a bad motivation at all. But I do think that it's sad to see the other kinds of values that get left behind. Having financial security is one way to take care of people, but having community and having a spiritual tradition are also ways to take care of people."—Jamie

"I have an ancestor who was named Edward F. Beale. He's my great great great uncle (or something.) He was the President of the Bureau of Indian Affairs out in California and he was responsible for putting a number of Indians on reservations. He then made millions of dollars off of land back in the 1850s. What I get from that is that he was making millions off of stolen land from Native Americans.

What I would love to do in my family is be able to trace all the different lines of where the money came from. I'd love to gather with other people with wealth and be able to tell our stories with a lot of analysis and make a case for reparations; to be able to really articulate to other people with wealth the ways in which—really literally—the wealth was stolen. To look at how labor was stolen from Chinese people and African American people and how this land was stolen from Native Americans. If we're talking about it from a white wealthy point of view, it might be less threatening to other white wealthy people because we're owning it rather than accusing from the outside.

My mother and my aunt keep saying stuff like, 'He wasn't such a bad guy, Edward F. Beale.' But I guess what I keep trying to articulate—both for them and for myself—is the difference between the institutional and personal. That, for instance, Edward F. Beale was part of a genocidal movement which he profited from, and within that he was an individual person who had relationships and feelings and was blind to what was going on, just like all of us at certain times. The institutional piece doesn't cancel out the personal piece. And the personal doesn't cancel out the institutional."—Laurel

"The story of my parents' wealth is not all just about their individual will—so much else played into it. My dad was very poor, but he was extremely fortunate because he got an education at a Wat (a Thai Buddhist temple). He then passed the exams to get into Chulalongkorn, which is like the Harvard of Thailand. That's where he met my mother. My mother's side of the family owned some land, so they were better-off. My parents both became doctors.

They decided to move to the United States in 1971 in part because of all the political turmoil—it was an extremely tumultuous period in Southeast Asian history, and tensions between students and the Thai military were rising. It was only because the U.S. had changed its immigration laws in the 1960s that they were able to go—before that Asian immigration was extremely restricted. It was also easier for them because they were doctors and the law gave preference to professionals, scientists and artists.

My parents set up their own practice and they worked like crazy, so I hardly saw them. Then my dad started getting into the stock market, reading all these books and doing investments. That was how they built up a fairly significant amount of money.

With immigrant families, when one person makes it you get everyone else holding on to you. You get this money and then you are expected to support everyone—filial piety and all. I think it can get a little crazy with the power and the pressure of being in that privileged position. At the same time, there was a real starvation mentality, especially coming from my dad. I remember cutting napkins in half to save money and having really cheap clothes. I think my dad felt like if you act like you have a lot of money then you aren't really Thai anymore."—Noy

"My father inherited from his father and that money came from a few generations back when his family owned coal mills in western Pennsylvania. But what I'll really inherit will be from money that he earned in his own life as a lawyer.

Then on my mom's side I won't be inheriting money via her branch of the family, but I will be inheriting—similar to on my dad's side—a kind of social elite status and upper class attitude that comes in a pretty direct line from my mom's mom's branch of the family being descended from slave traders. That was back seven generations ago in Rhode Island. At that time, not the guy who I'm descended from, but his sons and their sons, a few of them made a huge fortune in the slave trade. I'm not in a direct line from those huge fortunes, most of which were spent within a few generations. So technically speaking I haven't inherited money directly from the slave trade. However, I have definitely inherited social class status. I think it's important to name that and notice that whether it's the slave trade or any other major financial success in business—even if the money disappears—people typically marry into other families with money. So for us, this 'normal' sense of old-money New England entitlement really settled in.

The process of naming my privilege and the slave trade history has been liberating in the sense that when it was a subconscious thing, the guilt was really strong. It's been a gradual process of saying, 'Okay, since I'm not inherently a bad person, and my people are really good-hearted people nowadays, then I can start to look at this more objectively,' and saying, 'well, this was what the history was and it was totally fucked up and now what am I going to do about it?'"—Katrina

writing a new money story

step 1: record the original

First, you'll need to write out the original version of your money story as it stands now.

step 2: look for gaps

In general, you're looking for places where you think there might be more to the story. Take a close look at any spots in the narrative where there's a focus on just one person's heroic actions or where wealth simply equals hard work plus brains. One of the clearest signs that there may be more to the story than meets the eye is if it includes a version of any of these time-honored phrases:

- Pulled self up by the bootstraps
- Made wise investment choices
- Through hard work alone/worked day and night
- Raw talent/sheer brains/always a smart one
- Rags to riches
- Self-made
- Came to this country with nothing but the clothes on their backs

step 3: research and revision

Now comes the hard part: researching the missing parts of the story. Depending on how old your money story is, this can mean some serious digging. Here's a list of some of the factors that often go into creating wealth but usually get left out of money stories. Hopefully it will give you some ideas of where to start looking.

- Connections
- Luck
- Inheritance
- Education
- Relationships with banks and investors
- Belonging to a privileged identity group
- Community support
- Family support

- Support from religious and cultural institutions
- Marriage
- Federal wealth building programs (like the Homestead Act or the GI Bill)
- Tax breaks, subsidies and grants
- Government connections and contracts
- Immigration status
- Status in country of origin
- The impact of historical forces that built wealth for some while taking it from others (like slavery or war)

CHAPTER 8

The Side Effects

he idea that being wealthy equals being the smartest, hardest-working and most deserving can have some pretty strange effects on our lives. Especially since it means that, as people with wealth, we're constantly being told *we're* the smartest, hardest-working and most deserving. This happens so often that no matter how cool and down-to-earth we are, it can end up seeping into our brains and influencing the way we act.

At RG we like to call this the Side Effects of class privilege. Except instead of making us woozy and unable to operate heavy machinery, these class privilege side effects can cause us to act like our needs are more important than anyone else's. Or to feel like we should always be in charge and that we always know the best solution for any problem. Unfortunately the Side Effects also don't take very long to emerge—they can kick in quickly even for those of us who have only recently become wealthy.

The Side Effects go deep. They are more than just an opportunity we have that others might not. They actually change the way we act and relate to people. They can even seep into our closest relationships. That's why looking at the Side Effects can be one of the hardest parts of understanding our class privilege.

Luckily we have the power to counteract their effects and change the way we act. Before we can do that, though, we need to be able to recognize what they look like. (Learning to laugh at them doesn't hurt either.) So here are a few of the most common Side Effects, brought to us today by the multitalented, all-animal cast of the Class Privilege Players...

the boss effect

The Boss Effect occurs when we automatically take charge or take a leadership role, no matter what the situation. Or we just act like we're the boss even if we're not. Sure, we may have amazing leadership skills. But we can't possibly be the right person for the job *all* the time.

the ivory tower effect

The Ivory Tower Effect happens when we assume that a privileged education means we know more than anyone who doesn't have one. It leads to valuing academic experience over life experience to the point that we refuse to consider the opinion of anyone who doesn't have a fancy degree. This effect can also cause us to see academic reports, theories and statistics as the only valid ways to understand something—to the total exclusion of people's lived experience and emotion.

the waffle effect

Having privilege often also means having a lot of options open to us. This effect happens when we get so overwhelmed by all those options that we end up being unreliable or unable to commit to just one thing. We forget to take into account that changing our mind or making a sudden shift in plans might be a real problem for others who are counting on us.

the space cadet effect

This effect happens when we don't take into consideration the impact we have on others, especially with our physical presence. This can include walking in and out of meetings at will, leaving in the middle of things or coming late, canceling at the last second and, in general, making decisions based solely on what is convenient for us. Taking good care of ourselves is absolutely essential, but we can still do that while being conscious of the effect we have on everyone else.

the stage hog effect

The Stage Hog Effect often pops up if we're collaborating with a group or gathering together other people's experiences for a project. It especially comes into play if we have a higher academic degree or more resources than the other people involved. We can end up feeling like having privilege is the same thing as being the smartest and most important, and therefore we're entitled to *all* the credit. Instead of just being proud of our hard work, we wind up hogging the spotlight.

the daddy warbucks effect

This effect happens when we "share" privilege without checking in with what the other person actually wants. Giving money or paying for things can be a generous, caring act. It can also make people feel disrespected or undermined when they aren't consulted about it first. This effect can cause us to assume we know best what everyone needs, and blocks us from opening up a dialogue and working out a plan that feels right to everyone involved.

the all-knowing activist effect

This one occurs when we assume that our political view is the only way to see things and everyone else is ignorant. We forget that our political view is also shaped in part by the privilege we have. What feels most important and most urgent to us may be very different from what feels most important and urgent to someone with less privilege. This effect can end up isolating us from the very people we need to be working together with for social change.

the "ice ice baby" effect

This one comes into play when we look down at anyone who shows emotion, particularly in "serious" places, like at work. We end up assuming intelligence and leadership can only exist alongside feelingless-cool, and that emotional knowledge is useless. We may even freeze *ourselves* out in an attempt to conform to this icy ideal.

the big idea effect

This happens when we assume that we're the biggest brains to ever have tackled a particular social change issue. Therefore our solution will obviously be the best! So we completely skip the step of talking to others who are working on the same issue and who could help us gain a deeper understanding of what's actually going on. We just jump right into using our own resources and connections to make our plan happen. The Big Idea Effect means we end up putting our ideas—and our ideas alone—into action without ever having to consult or collaborate with anyone else.

the always comfy effect

This effect occurs when we get out-
raged or upset that someone has made
us feel uncomfortable about having
privilege. We end up assuming that
our need to feel comfortable is more
important than anything else. This
effect often pops up if someone asks
us for money or calls attention to our
privilege when we are trying to keep it
quiet. Even though feeling uncomfort-

able is totally miserable, if we freak out and close off whenever someone brings up
the fact that we have privilege, we can end up completely isolating ourselves.

the side effects' strange adaptability

Many of these class privilege Side Effects are similar to the ways that other kinds of
privilege, especially white privilege, get acted out. In fact, the more kinds of privilege
we have, the more kinds of Side Effects we can end up with—and the harder it can
be to catch when we're playing them out.

Another strange thing about the class privilege Side Effects is that almost everyone
with wealth in the United States comes down with them, no matter who they are.
People of all genders, races, ethnicities, cultures, religions, sexualities and abilities
can, with enough class privilege, end up acting out these same behaviors. Of course
our background and identity shape both the way we do it and how others respond
to us. Still, the general gist is almost uncannily the same.

Experiencing class privilege Side Effects is probably not the kind of thing we can
all get excited about having in common. It does say something though about the
power of class privilege to sneak its way into how we act no matter who we are or
where we come from. This means it won't always be easy to stop ourselves from
doing this stuff. But as long as we're willing to learn from our mistakes—and help
each other out—we have a pretty good shot.

thinking about Side Effects

■ Has someone ever pointed out to you that you were acting in a way you didn't even realize? How did it feel?

■ Can you think of a time when you acted out a class privilege Side Effect?

■ Did you notice how it impacted other people? Describe what it was like.

■ How does your identity shape the way you experience the class privilege Side Effects? Are there ways that your gender, race, ethnicity, culture, religion, sexuality, ability or other identities shape the way you might act them out?

■ Have you ever felt like the Side Effects were undermining a close relationship? Were you able to talk about this with the other person? What was this like?

■ Have you seen other people with class privilege act out Side Effects in the communities you are a part of? In what ways?

"We get stuck in our patterns and I think it's a big deal for individuals to break out of their family traditions and community traditions. I'm interested in having role models of people who do that. What does it take for them to do that? How can we really support each other? Because in our hearts we want to be a part of changing the status quo. It hurts us to be isolated and to know that we are holding resources that could make a big difference to other people." —Laurel

CHAPTER

Playing a Supporting Role

We're almost up to the part about taking action. Pinkie swear—look ahead a few pages, it's the truth. There's only one last big question left to wrestle with: What do we know about creating social change in the first place?

In some ways, we know a lot. Our experiences have given us an inside view into how class privilege keeps the unjust distribution of resources going. However, our experiences with privilege can also limit what we're able to see.

the more privilege we have, the harder it is to see the big picture

There's an exercise called "the privilege walk" that's sometimes done in diversity workshops. Everyone in the room starts out standing in the same place. Then the workshop leader asks questions about peoples' experiences with privilege and discrimination. Answer "yes" to having had an experience with privilege and you step forward. Answer "yes" to having had an experience with discrimination and you step back. As the exercise goes on, the people with more privilege end up towards the front of the room. Meanwhile, the people who have struggled economically, who have had to deal with things like racism, sexism and homophobia, end up towards the back of the room.

At the conclusion of the exercise the workshop leader asks, "Who in the room has the clearest view of what's going on?" The people with the most privilege, who have taken the most steps forward, can see only what's in front of them. (Which is usually just the wall or some macaroni art from the community center's afterschool program.) On the other hand, the people standing further back see the whole room and everyone in it.

The most effective social change leadership will always come from those who have the clearest vision. The more privilege we have, the harder it is for us to see what's going on. This means we're often not the best choice for a leadership role. We *can* learn to see beyond our own experiences. (Who wants to stare at macaroni art all day anyway?) All we have to do is turn around and start listening to everyone else in the room. Yet as much as we can learn, we won't ever know what it's like to stand in a less privileged place. We won't ever have the life experiences we'd need to see the big picture with the most clarity.

This doesn't mean we have to sit the whole thing out. There's still so much that each of us can bring to movements for social change. It's just that sometimes we've got to learn to take a supporting role instead of a leading one. While this is a real reversal from everything we've been told about young people with wealth being the future leaders, it's also our chance to become a more integral part of the change we seek.

the more privilege we have, the less our lives depend on change

Class privilege allows us to choose whether or not we want to work towards a fairer distribution of resources. If we don't take action, we will still have the resources we need. If we take action and fail, we will have resources to weather the consequences. If we decide things are getting too rough or we're too busy, we can drop out without sacrificing our chance for a better life. In fact, as long as we don't challenge the current set-up, having class privilege means that it will simply keep working in our favor.

We even get to choose whether or not we want to acknowledge our privilege in the first place. There's certainly a downside if we *don't* acknowledge it: we don't give ourselves the chance to understand a large part of our experiences, and that can really mess with our relationships and our lives in general. Still, being part of a privileged group means we are never forced by those in power to identify ourselves. We never have to join together with others like us to fight for our rights or to protect ourselves.

No matter how deeply we are committed to change, because we have privilege, our lives don't *depend* on it. Taking action is a choice, not a necessity. We can still make working for social change an utmost priority in our lives, for the rest of our lives. But if we want to be effective, we must learn to listen, support and take our lead from those who most urgently need things to change.

thinking about our role in social change

- What do you think are the most urgent priorities for change right now? How might class privilege affect your perspective on this?

- Are there ways that class privilege has helped you better understand social change? Are there ways that class privilege has made it harder to understand social change? How so?

- Are you currently taking a leadership role in any social change work? If so, are there ways that your experiences with class privilege might impact your effectiveness as a leader?

- What are some of the differences you've noticed in how it feels to take a leadership role versus a supporting role in social change work?

"The question of taking leadership in organizations is one that I struggle with a lot—knowing when it's appropriate for me to take leadership, and challenging myself not to. On the one hand, I need to have faith in the fact that I do know things and I do have a lot to offer in organizations that I'm a part of. On the other hand, I can't deny that my speaking up or taking leadership is problematic at times, or does take the space away from other people." —Nicole

Welcome to the Taking Action Section

Working to understand our own privilege can be hard. Being more open about it with people isn't easy either. The more we learn, the more we realize just how deep the unjust distribution of resources goes. Sometimes it's tough to see a bright side.

There is a bright side though. Our work can lead up to something pretty great: using our privilege for social change. So welcome to Part II: Takin' Action—everything you loved about Part I plus even more car chases and celebrity cameos.

Because each person's situation is so different, this part of the book is much more of a smorgasbord. The chapters ahead include both strategies for taking action and some big questions for thinking about the process behind it. There are also two snazzy fill-in-the-blank action plans to help you start mapping out your grand design.

Here's a quick overview, so you can skip around to the parts that are most relevant for you.

---

strategies for taking action with money
Chapter 10:
- o Socially responsible spending
- o Paying more/less taxes
- o Socially responsible investing

Chapter 11:
- o Giving

creating a money action plan
Chapter 12:
- o Action plan template and questions about how much is enough

strategies for taking action with privilege
Chapter 13:
- o Building a dialogue with people with wealth about social change, giving and investing
- o Challenging people with wealth when they act out class privilege stuff
- o Supporting and challenging other young people with wealth
- o Collaborating with social change groups on how to use our privilege

creating a privilege action plan
Chapter 14:
- o Action plan template and questions about the ethics behind using privilege

---

the taking action section ♥s the resource section

Many of these strategies are actually giant topics, and it would take a whole book to go into depth about most of them. Luckily for us, other people have already written those books! That's why there are lots of little nagging suggestions throughout this half of the book reminding you about the Resource Section. Think of the strategies here as appetizers: tasty, yes, but for more substantial fare, you'll need to do some research. The goal here is to get a broad view of the different actions we can take, and then focus on some of the trickier questions around privilege and power these strategies can raise.

types of strategies

The action strategies ahead break down into two main types. First there are strategies for using money. While some of us have class privilege without currently holding much cash, those of us who do have more money than we need can start putting it to work ASAP. In fact, most of these strategies don't actually require much money to put into action, so they may be worth reading up on anyway.

Next come the strategies for using privilege: these are all about how to use our networks, access and connections for social change. Most of these strategies aren't as activist-glam as going to a rally or organizing a protest, but they *are* some of the most effective ways we can use our resources for what we believe in.

lead? support? collaborate?

The last few chapters looked at why we need to watch out for always taking charge or assuming we always know what's best in any situation. This doesn't mean that, as people with privilege, we should *never* play a leading role in social change work.

One of the most powerful ways to build a dialogue about social change is to speak from common experience. This makes us perfect candidates for connecting with other people with wealth. Plus, people with wealth often grant those with similar privilege a special trust and authority, which gives us a chance to bring up challenging ideas that might otherwise get shut out. We're also the only ones who can take on tasks like moving our own investments, changing the way we spend or working together with our families and those closest to us.

Then there are situations where we've got to initiate taking action, but collaboration with others who have a clearer view of the social change big picture is crucial. For example, while only we can take the first step towards starting up our giving, creating a more collaborative decision-making process is a huge piece of the work ahead. While it's up to us to communicate with social change groups about the access and connections we have, it's through collaboration that we can figure out how to best put them to use.

How can we tell which situation is which? How do we know when to lead, when to collaborate and when to take a more supporting role? There's no quick and easy answer key for this one. Instead it's a question we have to be vigilant about asking ourselves throughout this work and throughout our lives. This stuff is just plain complicated, but as long as we're committed to the process, to keeping the lines of communication open and to learning from our mistakes, we'll be on the right track.

do we have to work with rich people?

Some of us grew up in wealthy communities where we were ostracized because we didn't fit in. Some of us grew up struggling economically and feeling angry at those with wealth, even if we now have money ourselves. For some of us, spending more time with rich people, even if it is in service of social change, feels like the opposite of the life we are trying to lead. So there are a bunch of reasons why working with people with wealth can be seriously low on our priority list, like, right after getting a million paper cuts and then dipping ourselves in lemon juice.

The problem is that avoiding other people with wealth doesn't erase our own class privilege. If we want to put that privilege to work for social change, there's no way around the fact that we'll have to spend some quality time with other rich people. To succeed, we'll need to find new ways of communicating with those who have privilege like us—without our anger, fear, sadness or judgment getting in the way.

but there's no way I can talk to...

Doing this work with the people closest to us, like family and childhood friends, can be intense, especially when we don't have a lot of values in common. These are the people who have the instruction manual on how to drive us crazy, even when we're just talking about what to eat for dinner. So how can we build a dialogue with them about something as emotional as social change?

While it ain't easy, this work also has the potential to transform our relationships in some amazing ways. Putting the time, effort and care into really communicating with people in our lives about what's important to us can end up making our relationships stronger and deeper in the long run. This isn't always true, and it's important to be realistic here about what people are capable of; otherwise we're setting ourselves up for a world of pain. If you feel ready to take a shot at it, though, you may just be surprised at what's possible.

but we've got so much more to offer than just privilege!

What about all the other ways we can take action for social change that have nothing to do with using money or privilege? What about the rest of our talents and skills, our passion and creativity? This section of the book isn't meant to imply that taking action with privilege is the *only* kind of action we should take. Just that it needs to be *a part* of the action we take. There's no reason why we shouldn't also be putting every last bit of our fabulousness to work for social change.

"My parents won the lottery when I was 18 years old. It was pretty amazing for my life to change overnight. How do you adjust to that? One of the biggest things is feeling a lot of responsibility and wondering if you're worthy or up to that responsibility and that blessing. Having grown up and not been personally very materialistic, it's kind of like, how can I live in this nice an apartment and still hold true to the values I felt I had before?

Why do I deserve not to have to worry about money as opposed to another person who has just as good a heart? I was afraid I might lose friendships. It became this really exciting, wonderful blessing, and at the same time it became this scary, isolating thing.

We need to come to terms with the fact that maybe we aren't any more worthy than the next person and maybe the sense of entitlement or lack of sense of entitlement doesn't need to exist and it centers on you doing the best in your situation. Usually when I hear people say I do the best with my situation—it's usually a situation that's at a disadvantage. When it's a situation that's at an advantage, it's a different kind of pressure—you don't want to mess it up. There's this extra fear of messing it all up, blowing the whole deal.

It's a real opportunity to truly do good, and so if your heart feels moved to do good and to work for change—try and use this opportunity. Do it without fear and without feeling ashamed. That's the best I can do."—Dawn

CHAPTER 10

Using Money for Social Change

Every little thing our dollars do affects the world around us. Even the simplest act, like, say, buying a bag of cheese puffs, links us up with the global economy. Where were the cheese puffs manufactured? How much did the people who made them get paid? How were the ingredients that went into them grown and produced? Once we start looking at the larger chunks of money we save and spend, there are tons of questions to think about...

strategy #1: socially responsible spending

There are a lot of people out there thinking about how we can best use our purchasing power to support social change. For example, the organization Co-op America has a bunch of great materials that cover pretty much the whole topic. Might as well just put this book down and check out their website at www.coopamerica.org.

Having extra cash can make it easier to be a more responsible consumer. We can afford to buy that organic kitty litter, even if it costs more. We've got access to reliable transportation, which makes it easier to travel a few extra miles to the unionized grocery store. The added expense and inconvenience of avoiding a boycotted product isn't such a big deal.

While there's no downside to using our buying clout for social change, it does bring up some deeper questions about class privilege. We can't forget that it's our privilege that enables us to make many of these choices. Privilege gives us a high level of control over how we live and what we buy, as well as giving us more free time to plan it all out. Until there's a more just distribution of resources, options that should be available to everyone—that could help everyone lead healthier lives on a healthier planet—will remain a luxury.

strategy #2: paying more/less taxes

People with wealth who believe in social change tend to have rather severe reactions to taxes. Either they're super-committed to paying *less* in the name of social change or they're super-committed to paying *more* in the name of social change.

The most extreme example of avoiding taxes for social change is war tax resistance. War tax resisters flat-out refuse to pay part or all of their taxes as a protest against government spending on war and weapons. As an act of civil disobedience, war tax resisting can land you in jail.

Estate planning, on the other hand, is the name of a perfectly legal way of avoiding taxes. Estate planning in general is about setting up and distributing assets in ways that conserve wealth and avoid taxes. However, many people use its strategies specifically for social change purposes. For example, they place their assets into trusts and foundations with social change giving missions to prevent those funds from being taxed. The idea behind this is that instead of the money going towards government expenses they don't agree with, it will all go to the social change causes they believe in.

Then there are the wealthy people who spend their time lobbying to pay *more* taxes. Groups like Responsible Wealth fight to keep wealth redistribution taxes, like the estate tax, in place and speak out about tax breaks that solely benefit the wealthy. While they may not agree with everything the government spends money on, they still believe that a fairer tax structure could mean more prosperity for more people.

So how do we decide which camp we're in when tax-time rolls around? One thing to keep in mind is that strategies like estate planning are based on the idea that wealthy people know best how to redistribute their money, and that no one else should have the power to tell them how to do it. Whereas the fairer taxes strategy is based on the idea that we should allow a democratically elected government to redistribute wealth. While our current government may do things that we adamantly oppose, it seems difficult to imagine that keeping control over wealth solely in the hands of the wealthy will ever lead to a more just distribution of resources.

strategy #3: socially responsible investing

Odds are that if we have some savings, they're not stored under our mattress but kept instead in investments. And while these investments may be profitable, the profits can come as a result of business practices and policies that don't fit with our social change values. The bank that gave us that swanky toaster may also have some creepy loan practices. The seemingly harmless cupcake company we hold stock in may also be polluting the local groundwater.

Luckily there's a whole field called Socially Responsible Investing (SRI)* we can look to for assistance on this. SRI's mission is to help investors make financial decisions that take social change values into account.

There are three main strategies to SRI:

Screening means setting up social change criteria that specifies what kind of companies to invest in and what kind of companies to avoid.

---

* See the Social Investment Forum at www.socialinvest.org for more about how SRI works.

Community Investing means investing in low- and middle-income communities both in the U.S. and in other countries. It's typically done by moving money into special banks or funds that then make loans for community development projects like building affordable housing and starting up small businesses. Some of the financial institutions that specialize in this kind of investing include community development banks, credit unions and community development loan funds.

Shareholder Advocacy means using the power of being a shareholder to affect the way a company operates. While screening can lead to selling off or donating stocks from companies that don't match up with our values, shareholder advocacy means holding on to those stocks in order to pressure the company to change its policies. Shareholder Advocacy can include actively voting our proxies*, joining together with other shareholders to file resolutions, opening a direct dialogue with corporate management and speaking to the press.

There are a ton of books out there about SRI. (See the Resource Section for a starter list.) And keep in mind that it doesn't take big bucks or owning stock to participate in socially responsible investing. Moving a small checking account to a community development bank or credit union makes a difference too.

what if i don't have control over where the money is invested?

When we're not the sole decision-makers over investments, taking action often means gearing up for a debate. Whether the money is part of a family business' investments, a foundation's endowment or a trust, there's usually a financially legit case to be made for SRI—though it can take some work to put it together. Thankfully, SRI is an industry, not just three hippies on a commune with a computer. So if the situation calls for some intimidating-looking statistics or a charming fancypants advisor, it's no problem. It can also help to remember that even if moving investments is out of the question, shareholder activism is often still an option. And check out Chapter 14 for ideas on how to start the conversation in the first place.

---

*Voting proxies means voting on proposals at a shareholder meeting by absentee ballot instead of being there in-person.

"Right now, I'm not sure that my lifestyle is fitting in with my own sense of what justice means to me, so I have to re-evaluate that. Initially when I came into this wealth from working at a dot com, there was a lot of guilt.

It's weird to go through this upwardly mobile process because people, even some of my close friends who I really love, don't totally get me. I've been feeling like, man, I'm not really part of the solution. I am not contributing to the world that I want to contribute to. I am just going around and buying all this shit and sometimes it really gets me down. So I'm struggling with that, finding some sort of balance in these two worlds.

I've talked to my folks a little bit about it. I think they're excited for me on some levels, but it doesn't compute for them. Here we are, we've been working our asses off for all our lives and now our son has so much money he doesn't have to work at all. In my family, we really define ourselves by what we do. So I'm in this weird box that they can't figure out.

I don't ever feel like I've earned this money. Having this money is somehow the way the economy worked for some weird period of time. Because of that, I've been given more resources than other people, so I have to use those resources to make the world a better place."—Bryce

creating an investment screen

If you're looking into screening your investments, a good first step is to create your own screen. A screen is a list of the criteria you use to determine what kind of companies to invest in and what kind of companies to avoid. Sometimes it also includes a statement of your values or your overall mission for investing.

Putting together a screen will make it easier to communicate your values to a financial advisor or any other person who works with you on investments. It will also leave you with a handy dandy value statement to share with other people you're trying to get inspired about SRI. Here are a few examples of common screening criteria and some questions to help you get started.

examples of common screens

I seek to invest in companies that:
- Pay living wages and good union relations
- Support racial justice
- Offer family-friendly and domestic partner benefits
- Have ecologically sustainable practices
- Support renewable energy
- Support community development
- Support access to healthcare
- Support international sustainable development
- Have gender equity in pay and benefits

I will not invest in companies that:
- Use child labor or sweatshop labor
- That have a history of discrimination
- Use animal testing
- Practice predatory lending
- Have excessive executive compensation
- Funnel money to oppressive governments abroad
- Are military/defense contractors
- Pollute the environment

questions

- What research do I need to do to help me create my screen?
- Who can help me with this and give me more ideas?
- What kinds of companies do I want to invest in?
- What kinds of companies do I want to avoid?
- What are some of my goals for my investments? How would I describe my investing mission?

finding an advisor

There's tons of advice out there about how to find a good financial advisor. However, there's not a lot on figuring out whether an advisor will respect your commitment to social change or if they work well with young people. So if finding an advisor ends up on your action plan to-do list, here are some ideas and questions that might be helpful.

■ Research is a great way to find out who's out there, but you'll also want to *get a referral* from at least one person who has worked with the advisor before. In general, you want to talk to some other people who've been there, done that, and get their advice.

■ If you have a few potential names, you might want to *have a phone consultation first* before taking the time to meet in person. Don't forget to ask if they have a minimum account size (to see if you're in their range) and how they charge their fees. This is also a good time to ask if they've worked with young people before and get a sense of how they react to your social change goals.

■ Once you've decided on someone you think you like, *set up an interview*. This part can feel intimidating if you've never done this before, so remember to come prepared with questions you want to ask. While you're there, make sure to take a good look around the office. Who else works there? Are there any young people around? Do they have a commitment to diversity? What are their written materials like? Do they make assumptions about your life and your goals that don't fit with who you are? Remember that you only need to share as much information about your finances as you are comfortable with. On the other hand, the more info you can share, the more accurate the advice you'll receive.

■ If someone doesn't click with you or if their approach turns you off, *keep looking*. Don't let anyone pressure you with a hard sell. You want an advisor who will be your ally, not someone who you're going to be uncomfortable talking to.

some sample interview questions

■ What's your experience working with people my age? How many of your clients are under 35? Can you give me the names of some of the young people you've worked with that I can call for references?

■ What is your investment philosophy?

■ How would you define your style of working with clients?

■ What do you like about your job?

- What areas of investments or financial planning do you specialize in?

- How often do you typically meet with your clients, and how easy is it to get in touch with you?

- How committed are you to educating your clients if they want to understand more about their finances? How have you helped clients in the past?

- Please tell me more about the process you go through with a client to develop a financial plan and/or give investment advice.

- What does socially responsible investing mean to you?

- What percentage of your clients use SRI strategies? Do you help them create screens? Do you help them do community investing? Shareholder activism?

- Tell me what you think are some of the best socially responsible investing options for me and why.

CHAPTER 11

Giving

One of the main ways to use money for social change is to give some of it away. The act of giving itself is pretty simple: just hand a few bills over to someone else or sign a check, and, boom, it's done. It's the decision-making process, the whole who-where-what-when-how of it, that's complicated. And once you throw class privilege into the mix, the whole thing gets even thornier. Here are some ideas on how to navigate it all.

avoiding strings

Some gifts are given entirely without strings. Like, "Hey buddy, you look hungry, have a sandwich." Some gifts are given with many, many strings attached. More like, "Hey buddy, you look hungry. I'll give you a sandwich as long as you can prove that you haven't eaten for two days, that you will effectively digest all parts of the sandwich, and that you will send me a progress report within a week detailing how you made use of the energy provided by said sandwich."

No one ever wants to feel like a gift was wasted or like it was a bad decision to give it in the first place. So sometimes we can end up attaching strings like restrictions and reports to reassure ourselves. Unfortunately, those strings also send a message of mistrust.

If we trust people enough to give them the money in the first place, we need to also trust that they know best how to use it. After all, they're the ones doing the actual work we're supporting, so they have the day-to-day experience it takes to know what's most needed. By giving without strings, we respect the knowledge of those we give to.

some obvious questions

Pointing out that it's a good idea to ask things like, "What do you need?" or "How can I help?" may seem obvious to the point of silly. After all, how else are we supposed to know what's needed? Yet, oddly enough, it's not common giving practice. Donors often assume that they already know what's best and never even open up a dialogue. So it's worth reminding ourselves from time to time that to be effective givers we also have to be effective communicators.

knowing what we don't know

Having class privilege can make it harder for us to see the big social change picture. (See Chapter 9 for more on this.) So if we really want to help create change through our giving, it's crucial that we work together with those who have a clearer view on all this.

In fact, no matter what the issue or area we're giving to, there are activists out there who have committed their entire lives to trying to make that change happen in their community—who know the histories, the strategies and the priorities inside and out. We don't have to have all the answers. We *don't* have all the answers. That's where collaboration comes in.

There's a whole range of ways we can make our giving processes more collaborative. We can rely on activist advisors to help us make decisions or share the decision-making power with us. We can give through funds that rely on experienced activists to decide where the money goes. (See the Resource Section for more on funds like this.) The kind of process we choose depends on how much control we're willing to share.

The "Making Decisions" exercise at the end of this chapter has a lot more on how to get started with this.

who benefits?

There's a saying that the rich only give to what benefits them, and, while that's a snarky way to put it, there's some truth there. The bulk of things rich people tradi-tionally give to—like universities, medical research and cultural events—*do* benefit wealthy communities. Even when funding other issue areas, wealthy people usually tend to give to groups that are run and controlled by those with class privilege.

While this kind of giving may be generous, it will never create a more just distribu-tion of resources. In order to do that, we need to focus on how we can move money *from* communities that have more than they need *into* communities that have less than they need. And once that money moves, it's essential that the people who live in the community have control over how it's used. Otherwise we're still keeping the real power in the hands of people with privilege.

what does success look like?

Our experiences with privilege can sometimes leave us with a peculiarly limited idea of success. We assume it will be easy to see: blue ribbons and perfect pie charts, lauded surveys and studies. But social change doesn't work like that. It's messy and slow and difficult to measure. Those kinds of evaluations only show us a fraction of what's going on.

That's why we need to ask the groups we're giving to what *their* visions of success look like. We need to understand how they evaluate their own progress both short- and long-term. Setting our benchmarks based on their vision can help us steer clear of the whole pie chart obsession and gain a broader view of what change-in-progress looks like.

failure schmailure

Social change isn't just one steady upward climb—it's ups *and* downs. If we're committed to supporting social change, we can't be afraid of failure.

Organizations and initiatives we give to will fall apart. Movements will flounder. Leaders will screw up. There will inevitably be all kinds of backlashes, chaos and even corruption. That doesn't mean that everyone involved wasted their time. What looks like a disaster in the short-term can often lead to long-term success. In fact, sometimes the most transformative movements and most talented leaders are born out of past failures.

It can also help to remember that our success as givers isn't tied to the success of those we give to. Our own success is about process, about communication, collaboration and challenging ourselves. It's about being a part of movement-building and working towards a more just distribution of resources. While we can't control the ups and downs of social change, we can always learn new ways to be better donors.

different forms

While there are special rules for charities, there aren't any restrictions on who individuals can or cannot hand their cash over to. Some non-profit organizations are certified by the government, which means that giving to them is tax deductible. Other kinds of giving may not save us on taxes but may still be just as meaningful. From political campaigns to collection plates, international coalitions to grassroots groups, family overseas to strangers on the street—social change giving takes on all kinds of different forms.

being open about our giving

Many of the ideas in this chapter rely on some pretty open communication about our giving and having wealth in general. Besides the usual stuff that can freak us out about this (check out Chapter 2 for more on that), there are two specific giving scenarios that tend to make most of us want to flee the premises.

First there's the "only-a-donor" scenario. Some people say that a person can either be a donor or an activist, but not both. So we worry that if we're out in the open about our giving, the rest of our social change work won't count anymore. Even if one minute ago we were activists working as part of a team, as soon as people know we're donors, our heads will be permanently replaced with giant money bags.

Then there's the "you're-a-saint" scenario. There's a style of fundraising that focuses on treating rich people like sagacious benefactors, even saviors, in order to persuade them to keep giving. Whenever the donor is around, everyone drops what they're doing to come show their infinite gratitude. This style also includes a multitude of gifts, lunches and honorary titles. So we worry that if the news gets out that we're donors, people will start treating us like this.

There are two ways to avoid ever having to deal with these scenarios. One is to never give. The other is to keep our giving a secret. Either plan means bowing out of some of the most effective ways to support social change through our giving—and out of the chance to build stronger, more trusting relationships across class lines. It'd be a lie to say these scenarios never happen in real life. However, they do happen a lot less frequently than we fear they will. And we do have the power to say "no thanks" to the creepy treatment or to point out that a person can be both a donor *and* an activist. Even though these scenarios can be kind of daunting, it still seems fair to say that the benefits of being open about our giving far outweigh the risks.

"Activist involvement is of the utmost importance in social change giving, in my view. It has to happen if there is to be true change—otherwise there is a power dynamic between the ones with the cash and the ones without the cash that hinders the work. I think that if a funder is truly dedicated to a shift in power, then that funder has to be willing to let go of the decision-making reins at some point."—Andy

transforming philanthropy

So what's the difference between philanthropy and giving in general? In the *Oxford English Dictionary*, it says philanthropy is an "effort to promote the happiness and well-being of one's fellow people." The word comes from the Greek "philanthropos" which literally means "love of people." By this definition, philanthropy is something that's been practiced around the world as part of pretty much every culture and every religion since humans have been keeping records. So obviously, access to *this* philanthropy isn't limited to those with class privilege.

Philanthropy is also the name of a specific institution in the United States. This philanthropy describes giving money (usually called "grants") through foundations. A foundation is a not-for-profit organization that is registered with the government and has to follow certain laws about how it operates, how much money it gives per year and who it can give it to. Philanthropy the institution is also dedicated to the common good, and sometimes it succeeds in that mission. However much of the decision-making power and control in philanthropy lies in the hands of those with wealth and privilege—which isn't so consistent with that whole common good thing.

Here are a few problems with the way philanthropy the institution currently works:*

- Very little grant money goes to progressive social change. One report found that less than three percent of funding in the United States goes to progressive social change.

- The people with decision-making power don't reflect the country's diversity. A national study showed that only 10 percent of foundation board members and only 2.2 percent of family foundation board members are people of color. (People of color make up 31 percent of the U.S. population, according to the 2000 census.)

- The process of applying for most grants is intimidating and overwhelming. Twenty page grant proposals are standard. You can't even apply to some foundations without being invited. Decisions are made behind closed doors and there's not usually any way to find out how or why a decision got made.

- Very few foundations rely on activists' expertise and experience when making their funding decisions.

---

* The statistic on social change funding is from the 1998 report "Social Change Grantmaking in the U.S." by the National Network of Grantmakers. The statistics on diversity in philanthropy are from the 2001 national study "Diversity Practices in Foundations" done by The Joint Affinity Groups of the Council on Foundations.

- Funding is often given with a lot of strings attached about what it can be used for and how it should be used.

- Private foundations, like family foundations, only have to give away five percent of their assets a year, and right now they can even deduct their operating expenses from that. Very few private foundations give away more than that five percent minimum each year. Meanwhile, the bulk of their assets sit in investments that may not even be in line with their own mission.

There is a whole movement of people who are trying to transform the institution of philanthropy and change some of these problems. Their work is often called "social change philanthropy." Some of their goals are:

- To make philanthropy more accessible and diverse.

- To change the way decisions are made so that activists who are actually working on the issues being funded are a part of the grant-making decisions.

- To ensure that more than three percent of funding goes to progressive social change.

- To build partnerships between foundations and the groups they fund instead of top-down relationships.

Lots of people with wealth are a part of this movement. Some of them even helped get it started. They're using their access to philanthropy to help push for change—and we can too. Class privilege can get us in the front door to many of the restricted-access organizations, conferences and events that shape the way philanthropy runs. Some of us even come from families that have foundations, giving us an even greater level of philanthropic access.

See Chapter 13 for more on ways we can use our access to help work towards institutional change. There's also a list in the Resource Section of organizations working on transforming philanthropy. And RG has a whole separate workbook for people trying to make change in their family's philanthropy that you can check out! (Just e-mail RG at info@resourcegeneration.org.)

"When you give money to a political action committee, as opposed to a non-profit, you can't be anonymous. Your name goes down on the list of funders for campaign finance law. When we finally turned in all the names—less than twelve hours after we turned that shit in—I got a call on my home phone from my local, major newspaper. They were like, 'We noticed that you gave a lot of money to the police accountability campaign, we want to talk with you.'

I was at a demonstration, surrounded by all these anarchists, punky kids who I thought would feel the most uncomfortable about my wealth, but they were like, 'Hey, are you the person who gave $25,000 to the police accountability campaign?' I was like, 'Yeah, man.' And they said, 'That's so great, man.' It was all positive.

I was expecting to get tons of phone calls from non-profits and every grassroots organization in Portland but I didn't. The one call I did get the same day the paper came out was from Tufts Alumni. I hadn't even been to Tufts yet. I was just planning on going to Tufts in the fall. It's so depressing. Who has the funding apparatus to jump on a newspaper article? Only the private universities. Most other organizations don't have the resources to do that.

But I've painted a far too positive picture of my whole attitude towards money, towards how I dealt with it. So I want to quickly run through why I think it's fucked up that I gave all that money to the police accountability campaign: I don't like being fundraised. I want to give money spontaneously when I see something I like. But that is totally disempowering for organizations. Organizations need money and they can't go out and search for me when they need money. You have to wait for me to stumble across you? What am I going to stumble across?"—Greg

"I was a volunteer at an organization that needed some resources in a very immediate term. I said, 'What if I were able to provide these resources?' Suddenly the group of people said, 'Are you sure you want to give us that money? How do you feel about that? Are you okay? Are we okay? Do we really want to be taking money from you?' Which I thought was very bizarre since 15 minutes before we'd just been having a conversation that went along the lines of: 'We don't care where we get the money, we just gotta get it from somebody. All we want is for some rich person to give us the money and then we'll be fine.'

As soon as the personal relationship entered the scene, people had a whole different set of criteria about whether or not they even wanted to accept the money. Did they want to have somebody so close to the organization also be a major donor? As a major donor would that person exert some demands for accountability that might result in agenda setting? If that person paid for the organization's rent for three months, did that mean that at the next meeting, when they were brainstorming ideas, that they would be expected to go with that person's ideas because they paid for the organization to exist?"—Holmes

"It was hard because our names are on the foundation's website. And so I would be volunteering at some non-profit and someone would come up to me and say, 'We were doing research for grants and we noticed that your name was on this website—we had no idea.' And it made me really resentful because I just wanted to be a normal volunteer. I didn't want to be a potential funder. I didn't want to be singled out, and it happened a lot. So I was very apprehensive about being on the board: I didn't want to be different, didn't want to be treated differently in the non-profit world.

But over time I got really excited about the possibility of what I could do. These were just the resources I had at hand and it was time to do something positive and not hide from it anymore. I just kind of said, 'It's time to get over this.' I mean money had been such an issue for me all my life. But I eventually re-conceptualized it in my head as an opportunity to make real change."—Rachel

making decisions

part 1: What's my current decision-making process?

(Skip this part for now if you haven't started giving yet)

1. What is my current giving focused on?

2. What was the process for deciding that focus?

3. The following people are involved in my current giving decision-making:

4. For each person listed above, answer the following two questions:

   ■ *How much control do they have over the decision-making?* Rate them on a scale of zero to five, with five being the most control and zero being no control. Keep in mind that someone who serves only as an advisor has much less control than the person who actually gets to make the decision, even if their advice significantly influences the outcome.

   ■ *How directly does the work being funded impact them?* Rate them on a scale of zero to five, with five being the most impacted and zero being not directly impacted at all. For example, imagine an affordable housing project being developed in a local neighborhood: someone who is neither working on the project nor living in the neighborhood would be a zero. Someone from the neighborhood who is also a leader in the project would be a five.

5. The goal here is to create a giving process where those who are the most impacted by the work being funded have at least as much control over decision-making as those who are less impacted. *Where is my current giving in relation to this goal?*

part 2: setting up a more collaborative process

Here are a few examples of ways to have a more collaborative process and the range of control and time commitment that comes with them:

■ *Less control, less time:* giving through a fund that relies on experienced activists to decide where the money goes. (See the Resource Section for more on funds like this.) Volunteering to help out at the fund is one way to feel more involved while still handing over the decision-making power.

■ *More control, more time:* asking activists to advise you on your giving, either at a formal meeting or informally over the phone. Less control would mean sharing the decision-making power together.

- *More control, less time:* Setting up a donor-advised fund at an activist-led foundation. Then basing some or all of your giving on the foundation's advice. (A donor-advised fund is a special account at a foundation that a donor can contribute into and then recommend how the money should be distributed.)

- *A little less control, more time:* Joining a giving circle that includes activists or is activist-advised. (A giving circle is a group of people who are pooling their giving resources together and making collaborative decisions. See www.givingforum.org/givingcircles for more info.)

Here are some questions that can help you figure out your next steps:

- How much time do I want to spend on my giving process?

- How large is the current scope of my giving? Am I setting up a process for just one year? For giving away a big chunk of assets? For a longer-term plan?

- How important is it to me that I *am* a part of the decision-making? How important is it to me that I *am not* a part of the decision-making?

- Am I directly impacted by the work I am funding? Am I giving back to a community that I come from? Or am I transferring resources to a community that I am not a part of?

- How does this affect my process and participation? How do my experiences with privilege and with discrimination affect my relationship to my giving?

- Are there funds or networks of funders that already focus on the work I want to support? Are any of these activist-led or activist-advised?

- Who do I know that is directly impacted by the work being funded and could help me with this process?

part 3: if you're asking for advice

If you are asking other people to help you as advisors or decision-makers, it's important to be respectful of their time. A short phone call or e-mail is one thing, but if they're going to be a part of a longer process or come to a meeting, here are some points to keep in mind:

- Offer a stipend or honorarium out of respect for the time they are spending.

- Be clear about how much decision-making power they will have. Are they giving advice or do they actually have some control over where the money goes?

- Explain upfront how much money there is to give, and whether or not the funding focus is up for discussion.

- If you are bringing together a large group of people, you may need a facilitator to help everyone get to know each other and set up a process for making decisions that everyone is comfortable with.

- If you are meeting together in person, be considerate of people's needs. Help with transportation and childcare. Find an accessible, safe and comfortable meeting place. Don't forget to have lots of food and make sure to ask if people have any special needs.

how do the groups you give to evaluate their work?

The first step to evaluating your giving in a different way is to learn more about how the groups you are giving to envision success. Here are a few questions that can help you find out more about this.

- What are some of the most important things the group has learned in the past few years about this work?

- What is the group's vision of short-term change? What about long-term change?

- What are some of their current goals?

- How does the group measure their success?

- What's their process for evaluating how things are going? Who is a part of this process?

- What are some of the challenges the group is currently facing?

- Does the group have an annual report, event or some other way that they share their progress with the community?

research tips

Here are some tips for learning more about a specific issue or area.

Some good ways to get started:

- Read local or issue-specific newspapers and newsletters.

- Include art, music, poetry, essays, film and biographies of activists as part of your research. Academic studies and statistics alone won't give you a full picture.

- Participate in events, meetings, festivals, protests or actions.

- Volunteer to help out at an organization.

The best way to learn more is to talk to the people who are doing the work.

Some good questions to ask:

- What inspires you to do this work?

- Tell me more about its history.

- What are the main causes of some of the issues you are working on?

- What strategies do you think have been the most successful in this work? What strategies have been the least successful?

- What are some of the barriers or challenges to doing this work?

- What are the most urgent current funding needs?

- What are some of the other groups that you work with?

- What is your vision of short-term change? Of long-term change?

As you learn more, here are some questions you'll want to be able to answer:

- Who are at least three groups working on this issue or within the area?

- What have you learned about each of these groups? Have you seen them in action?

- Who do the groups work with? Who do they represent? How are the people they represent involved in the organization and its decision-making?

- Are there differences in how each group sees their mission and vision for change? In their strategies?

- What other groups are they collaborating with? How well do you understand the coalitions and alliances between groups that work on this issue or in the area?

- Who are at least three community leaders or activists focused on this work? What have you learned about their visions for change?

- Where does funding for this work currently come from? What have you learned about current funding needs?

giving to family and friends

All the stuff in this chapter about respect, communication and collaboration being crucial elements of a giving process applies here too. In fact, multiply its importance by a thousand. Some people say that giving money to family or friends messes up relationships. But it's not the money itself that's the problem—it's the unspoken power issues that screw things up. A good rule of thumb is: if you can't talk about it together, it's probably not going to go too well. Here are some other tips based on the experiences of people involved with RG:

- *Come to an agreement together.* Surprises here are no good. You must work out all the terms together in a way that makes everyone involved feel heard and respected.

- *Consider giving a gift instead of a loan.* If the other person is more comfortable with it being a loan or you cannot afford to give it as a gift, never lend with interest. (The last thing you want is to be profiting off of the fact that someone you care about needs your help.) Or consider continuing the flow of resources by asking them to pass the loan on to someone else who needs it instead of paying it back to you.

- *Be clear about your own intentions.* Are you truly giving this without strings or are you expecting something in return? Are you going to be watching how they spend every penny and feel betrayed if they don't use it the way you think they should?

- *Consider setting up a collaborative loan fund or emergency fund* with friends or family. Everyone puts in what they can, and members of the group can each draw on it when they need to. Having enough in savings to weather an emergency is a big deal, and something we often take for granted as people with wealth. This is one way to share that advantage with others in your life. Again, the fund is still something you need to talk through creating and setting up together—it has to be a group process.

CHAPTER 12

Creating a Money Action Plan

And now...(insert exciting musical fanfare here) on to the action plan! A quick warning, though, before we rush in: making a money action plan isn't easy. Not that anything else we've done this far was easy. This part is just particularly hard, because to make a plan we've got to come up with actual, actionable numbers, and that's a whole process in itself.

Having more money than we need means we can base those numbers on our values instead of just necessity—and this is where all the tough questions come in. How do we know how much is enough? How much is enough for our own expenses? How much is enough to save? How much is enough to give away? How much is enough to earn? How much is enough to take care of the people who depend on us?

There's no simple equation. We can't use calculations like *(assets + income) - expenses = giving*. That only works when giving is an afterthought, not when it's a central part of our social change values.

Creating a plan is more like a balancing act, with our needs and responsibilities on one end and our commitment to supporting change on the other. Plus, planning our future expenses is extra tricky if we're not sure yet what sort of future we're aiming for. Really it's more like one of those acts where the guy is riding a unicycle and balancing a spinning plate on his head. It takes some practice.

So, first up: some thoughts and exercises that get at the big questions behind creating a plan. Then, at the end of the chapter, there's a template for making the plan itself.

do i have the skills i need?

Some of us already have pretty solid financial management skills. For those of us who feel a little shakier in this department, dealing with numbers can be intimidating. Our comfort level usually depends on the kind of financial education we've received up until now. While some of us were schooled in budgets and bonds from day one, many of us were never even taught how to write a check. Financial education also often breaks down along gender lines, even within the same family—while the men learn about money, everybody else just gets piano lessons.

Now's our chance to take our education into our own hands: rich kids with no financial skills, unite! Grab an equally clueless buddy and make a field-trip to the bookstore to get some stuff on economic literacy. Check out the Resource Section for a few ideas on where to start.

who can help me?

We don't have to do this work alone. There are so many people who can help us create our plans and put them into action. We can ask friends and family for support. We can sign on with professionals like financial advisors, lawyers and accountants. Asking for help and advice is a big part of putting together a doable money action plan.

Besides, we can't do this work alone even if we wanted to. Family, partners, kids, friends...anyone that we share a financial responsibility *with* or a financial responsibility *for* will need to be in on at least some of the conversations and decisions. And for those of us who don't have decision-making power over our resources, creating an action plan requires working with a whole other gang from relatives to trustees to investment managers. No matter who's involved, getting them all on board with the plan is essential to making it happen.

"I get really confused. My mom feels like, 'Oh my God, I didn't give you very much at all.' And compared to my relatives the fact that, in her eyes, I'm going to have to work in my lifetime embarrasses her. She never had to work for an income for herself. Then I turn around to my partner and she says, 'You don't have to work a day in your life! You can just live off this!' It's all these different messages. I haven't been able to really figure out a middle ground. They're such different realities."

— Charlotte

how much is enough to spend?

It's hard to make financial decisions if you don't have a sense of how much you spend per year. Some of us have spreadsheets, bar graphs and color-coded file folders. Some of us have a thing called "The Drawer" where we shove every bill, receipt and statement, and otherwise avoid its contents like the plague. If you've got "The Drawer" (or its even scarier cousin, "The Box"), don't worry. You can still get started on figuring out your annual expenses. The simplest way is to create a budget.*

If you've never written a budget before, here are some tips on how get started:

1. *Keep a detailed log of all your expenses for one month.* You've got to be very anal here and record everything, from credit card charges down to the receipt for a Snickers bar. (Low-tech notepads or high-tech PDAs—either will do the job, so use whatever you're most comfortable with.) By the end of the month you'll start to have a sense of both how much you spend and what categories of things you spend it on.

2. *Use your log to determine the budget's categories and expense estimates.* If you're feeling computer-savvy, now is a good time to start experimenting with a user-friendly accounting software program like Quicken. It's also a good time to set up a new filing system for future bills and statements.

3. *Here's a list of some common categories* to give you an idea of what your budget might include.

   - *Household:* rent or mortgage, utilities, phone, cable, insurance, food, maintenance.
   - *Financial:* taxes, fees for financial advisors or accountants, legal costs.
   - *Medical:* insurance, doctor and dental bills, medicine, therapy, alternative medicine.
   - *Entertainment/Travel:* vacations, books, music, movies, magazine subscriptions, gym, sports.
   - *Giving:* family and friends, community foundations, organizational memberships, non-profits, political contributions.

---

* Thank you to North Star Asset Management for the template this exercise is adapted from and for their help creating the workshop some of this chapter is based on.

■ *Education/Career:* tuitions, school loans, training, conferences, books and supplies, equipment.

■ *Transportation:* bus or subway pass, car expenses, bike expenses, insurance.

■ *Family:* child-care, long-term care for aging relatives, caring for pets.

■ *Personal care:* clothes, shoes, haircuts, toiletries.

4. *Start monitoring your expenses* to see how closely you're sticking to the budget. Are you over or under your estimates? Are you over because you spent too much or because you underestimated what you needed? Are there categories where you need to figure out how to spend less? Or more? After a few months of working on your budget, you'll begin to get a much clearer sense of what your annual expenses are.

5. *Check out the financial planning books* listed in the Resource Section for more information on how to pull this whole budget thing off. You may also want to look back at the section on socially responsible spending in Chapter 10, since the decisions you make about that will also affect your budget.

how much is enough to save?

While our current expenses are relatively knowable, predicting the future is a little trickier. How are we supposed to answer giant questions about family or career if we're living in a dorm eating ramen? And even if we do have it all mapped out, unexpected stuff happens all the time. There's no way we can know the exact amount of every expense we'll ever have for the rest of our lives.

However, it's still possible to make some long-term savings decisions, no matter how unsure we are about the road ahead. Big-ticket items like college tuitions and retirement costs can be estimated. Buying insurance can help with preparing for the unexpected.

Having a savings strategy is also a safeguard against the action-plan-shredding power of Questions of The Future. For example: "Don't you want your children to have the best educational opportunities possible?" Even if you *hate* kids, even if the last thing in the world you want is to raise a child, all of the sudden you can be seized with the feeling that you'd better sock aside as much money as humanly possible *just in case*. But with a clearer sense of what things actually cost in the long run, it's possible to calmly withstand Questions of The Future, and just evaluate our decisions accordingly.

Coming up with a savings strategy does require brainstorming a bit about plans and goals. The key is to get comfortable with feeling unsure instead of freaking out. You want to focus on creating a list of the possibles, whether it's raising chickens or running away with the circus. Don't sweat the details—you can sign up for trapeze lessons later.

Once you've got your list, you can move into research mode and start learning more about what different options cost. You'll need some help with this step, whether it's from financial planning books, websites or working with a socially responsible financial planner. (See the Resource Section for a few starter ideas.)

Okay, then. Step one: here come the brainstorming questions. Don't forget to breathe...

■ Where do I see myself living in the long run? Is it a goal to own my own home?

■ What are my transportation needs? How might these change in the future?

■ What kind of debt do I have right now? Do I have a long-term plan for managing it?

- What kind of work do I see myself doing? How might this affect my savings strategy?

- Do I see myself doing more school or more training in the future? Do I need to research tuitions or other training costs?

- Do I need to think about tuition costs for others in my life?

- What other things do I need to save for to help out the people I share my life with?

- Do I want to think about kids? Or helping out with raising the kids of family or friends?

- Do I need to think about taking care of aging relatives?

- How important is travel to me? Are there big trips I want to save for?

- What kinds of insurance policies might be relevant for me? (Some examples of insurance types: long- and short-term disability, medical, life, homeowner, renter, auto.)

- Is there money that others have put aside specifically for my long-term expenses? What will my access to these funds be? How should this figure into my planning?

- What about healthcare and health insurance?

- Are there medical expenses or surgeries that I need to save for?

- How can I plan ahead for taking care of emergencies? What kind of expenses do I know I'll need to be able to cover?

- What's my vision of being old and gray and retired? How do I imagine what my life will be like?

- What's my plan for figuring out wills and other legal stuff? Are there people who depend on me right now? Do I have things set up so that they'll be okay if something happens to me?

can we touch the principal?

You'd think it was something dirty, the way they talk about never touching the principal. Unfortunately, it's not that exciting: the principal just means the original amount of money invested as opposed to the interest or income that comes from that money. That's why if our only goal is to grow and preserve wealth, the mantra of never touching the principal makes sense. As long as we don't dip into the original investment, our starting level of wealth is maintained in perpetuity.

Of course, our goal here is a more just distribution of resources. So why shouldn't we at least consider touching the principal? Here are some questions to help break the taboo.

- How important is it to me to grow my assets? How come?

- How important is it to me to preserve my assets at their current level? How come?

- How important is it to me to decrease my assets? How come?

- How important is it to me that my investments support social change? What if that means my investments just hold steady but don't grow? What if that means they decrease in value?

- What do I think about passing wealth on to the next generation? To those who depend on me? Do I believe in inheritances? Is there a limit as to how much is too much? Or too little?

- How can I balance supporting those who depend on me with supporting a more just distribution of resources?

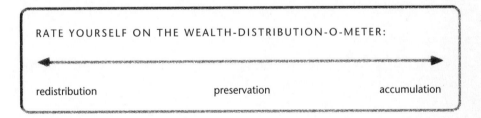

RATE YOURSELF ON THE WEALTH-DISTRIBUTION-O-METER:

redistribution   preservation   accumulation

thinking about security

Finances play a big part in our sense of security. Since our government doesn't provide much of a financial safety net for anyone, having enough savings can mean the difference between being able to make it through hard times and falling into debt.

On the other hand, no dollar amount can provide total security. Like they say at the protest march, "no justice, no peace"—until we live in a more just world, we're always going to be on red alert. Security is also an emotional state, and there's not enough money on the planet to make us feel safe if we are overwhelmed by fear or mistrust or are coping with trauma.

The trick here is to make our financial decisions based on a realistic idea of security. Otherwise, even the richest rich person can end up feeling like they'll never have enough.

Here are some questions that can help with thinking about security:

- What is my ideal vision of security in my own life? What kind of a role does money play in that vision? What else plays a role in that vision?

- What is my ideal vision of security for all people? What kind of a role does money play in that vision? What else plays a role in that vision?

- What makes me feel in danger or like I do not have what I need? How much of a factor is money in offsetting that feeling?

- How do my experiences with privilege and with discrimination affect the way I understand security?

how much is enough to earn?

This can be a particularly complicated question if we have more money than we need. Some of us have enough in the bank to make earning an income optional. Some of us need to earn our income, but have enough money to broaden our options—whether it's the freedom to work fewer hours, choose a career that pays less, or just say, "Take this job and shove it," without worrying about how we'll get by until we find another.

The choices we make about earning have a huge impact on our saving, spending and giving decisions, and on how we set up our money action plans in general. So here are some questions to help break it all down. For the sake of simplicity: "Moolah" = the money that's more than you need, either accumulated savings or an inheritance. "Earnings" = the income you earn through your work.

- Do you rely on the moolah for your current day-to-day expenses?

- Do you feel differently about your earnings than you do about the moolah? Do you use the two differently?

- Are there larger, long-term expenses you rely on the moolah for? (Like buying a home or vacations or emergencies?)

- Do you have total control over the moolah? If not, who else has the control? If you don't have control, how does that affect the way you use it and the way you feel about it?

- If you use the moolah for your living expenses, would your lifestyle be different if you lived entirely off what you earned? How much would you need to earn a year to live a similar lifestyle to the one you live now?

- Do you currently have a job? Is it a paying job or a non-paying job? Do you work for someone else or are you self-employed? Do you work full-time or part-time? How does your work—and what you earn from it—affect the way you feel about yourself?

- If you earned more, would it change the way you make decisions about the moolah?

- Does the moolah allow you to pursue an occupation that may provide less income but is more in line with your social change values? Or with your dreams or aspirations?

- Have you made career or school choices based on the assumption that you would be able to support or supplement your income with the moolah?

■ Has the moolah helped allow you to start a new business or organization? Do you still rely on that money to keep the business running?

■ Does the moolah enable you to volunteer or spend more time on your activism? What is the difference between supporting a movement through giving and supporting your own expenses so you can participate more fully in that movement?

how much is enough to give?

If there's a price-tag on that snazzy, more just world in the store window, none of us have the cash to cover it on our own. (Though if a big enough group of us chipped in…) While we can figure out saving and spending based on what stuff actually costs, we can't really calculate our giving that way.

Some religions have a tithe or a percentage of income that all members of the faith must give away each year. This is one guide that people use for choosing how much to give. Some people come up with their own percentage based either on their income or their assets. There's a big range here: some of us aim to give away 50 percent of our assets. Some of us aim to give away five percent of our income.

That said, the answer to this question might be the simplest of any in the chapter. How much is enough to give? As much as we can.

"One goal I have is to get in the practice and habit of giving. Another goal is to push myself to be uncomfortable in my giving and feel like I'm maybe giving more than I should." — Justine

what do i have?

Having more accurate information about our resources can make action planning a lot easier. If you need to do some research on what you have, the following exercises can help you get started.

Keep in mind that the money doesn't have to be all in your own bank account. If your money comes from your family, you might want to think about what access your family has as a whole. And while things like trusts or family foundations might have restrictions on how those funds can be used, don't forget that you may still have influence over how they are invested or given away.

If you're not ready for research-mode yet, don't let that stop you from making an action plan! Just base your plan on whatever you *do* know—you can always add to it later.

part 1: where to start looking?*

accounts and stuff

CASH

☐ Yes and I know how much: _____   ☐ Yes, but I don't know how much
☐ I need to research this   ☐ Definitely not

CHECKING ACCOUNT

☐ Yes and I know how much: _____   ☐ Yes, but I don't know how much
☐ I need to research this   ☐ Definitely not

SAVINGS ACCOUNT

☐ Yes and I know how much: _____   ☐ Yes, but I don't know how much
☐ I need to research this   ☐ Definitely not

MONEY MARKET ACCOUNT

☐ Yes and I know how much: _____   ☐ Yes, but I don't know how much
☐ I need to research this   ☐ Definitely not

CD

☐ Yes and I know how much: _____   ☐ Yes, but I don't know how much
☐ I need to research this   ☐ Definitely not

---

* This exercise is adapted from the book *Robin Hood Was Right: A Guide to Giving Your Money for Social Change* by Chuck Collins, Pam Rogers and Joan Garner.

140

BROKERAGE ACCOUNT

☐ Yes and I know how much: _____   ☐ Yes, but I don't know how much
☐ I need to research this   ☐ Definitely not

MUTUAL FUND

☐ Yes and I know how much: _____   ☐ Yes, but I don't know how much
☐ I need to research this   ☐ Definitely not

INVESTMENT IN A BUSINESS

☐ Yes and I know how much: _____   ☐ Yes, but I don't know how much
☐ I need to research this   ☐ Definitely not

HEDGE FUND

☐ Yes and I know how much: _____   ☐ Yes, but I don't know how much
☐ I need to research this   ☐ Definitely not

COMMUNITY LOAN FUND

☐ Yes and I know how much: _____   ☐ Yes, but I don't know how much
☐ I need to research this   ☐ Definitely not

BONDS (LIKE TREASURY BILLS OR SAVINGS BONDS)

☐ Yes and I know how much: _____   ☐ Yes, but I don't know how much
☐ I need to research this   ☐ Definitely not

STOCK CERTIFICATES (NOT IN AN ACCOUNT)

☐ Yes and I know how much: _____   ☐ Yes, but I don't know how much
☐ I need to research this   ☐ Definitely not

INSURANCE POLICY (THAT YOU ARE THE BENEFICIARY OF)

☐ Yes and I know how much: _____   ☐ Yes, but I don't know how much
☐ I need to research this   ☐ Definitely not

LIMITED PARTNERSHIPS

☐ Yes and I know how much: _____   ☐ Yes, but I don't know how much
☐ I need to research this   ☐ Definitely not

REAL ESTATE

☐ Yes and I know how much: _____   ☐ Yes, but I don't know how much
☐ I need to research this   ☐ Definitely not

LOANS OWED TO YOU

☐ Yes and I know how much: _____   ☐ Yes, but I don't know how much

☐ I need to research this   ☐ Definitely not

RETIREMENT ACCOUNTS

☐ Yes and I know how much: _____   ☐ Yes, but I don't know how much

☐ I need to research this   ☐ Definitely not

CAR

☐ Yes and I know how much it's worth: _____

☐ Yes, but I don't know how much it's worth   ☐ Definitely not

HOME

☐ Yes and I know how much it's worth: _____

☐ Yes, but I don't know how much it's worth   ☐ Definitely not

OTHER BIG STUFF (FOR EXAMPLE: BOATS, JEWELRY, ART)

☐ Yes and I know how much it's worth: _____

☐ Yes, but I don't know how much it's worth   ☐ Definitely not

trusts

TRUST

☐ Yes and I know how much: _____   ☐ Yes, but I don't know how much

☐ I need to research this   ☐ Definitely not

WHAT KIND OF TRUST IS IT? _____

(For example: revocable trust, irrevocable trust, bypass trust, generation skipping trust, charitable remainder trust, or charitable lead trust.)

WHO MAKES DECISIONS ABOUT MY ACCESS AND INVESTMENT?

☐ I do   ☐ My trustees and I do   ☐ Only my trustees

WHO ARE THE TRUSTEES?

☐ I know them, they are: _____

☐ I need to research this

WHAT KIND OF ACCESS DO I HAVE?

☐ Access to principal   ☐ Access to distributions   ☐ No access

HOW WILL MY ACCESS CHANGE BASED ON CONDITIONS IN THE TRUST?

(For example: age, life events, career choice…)

☐ Won't change   ☐ Will gain limited access

☐ Will gain full access   ☐ My children will gain access

WHAT ARE THOSE CONDITIONS IN THE TRUST? _____

access to philanthropy

FAMILY FOUNDATION

☐ Yes and I know how much the foundation gives away per year: _____

☐ Yes, but I don't know how much   ☐ I need to research this   ☐ Definitely not

What's my role? _____

(For example: trustee, junior board member, or potential decision-maker.)

OTHER CHARITABLE VEHICLES (FOR EXAMPLE, A DONOR ADVISED FUND)

☐ Yes and I know how much is given away per year: _____

☐ Yes, but I don't know how much   ☐ I need to research this   ☐ Definitely not

What's my role? _____

(For example: decision-maker or potential decision-maker.)

income

I have an income through my job:

☐ Yes and I know how much: _____   ☐ No

I have regular income from investments:

☐ Yes and I know how much: _____   ☐ Yes, but I don't know how much

☐ I need to research this   ☐ Definitely not

debt

MORTGAGE

☐ Yes and I know how much: _____   ☐ Yes, but I don't know how much

☐ I need to research this   ☐ Definitely not

SCHOOL LOANS

☐ Yes and I know how much: _____ ☐ Yes, but I don't know how much
☐ I need to research this   ☐ Definitely not

CREDIT CARD DEBT

☐ Yes and I know how much: _____ ☐ Yes, but I don't know how much
☐ I need to research this   ☐ Definitely not

CAR PAYMENTS

☐ Yes and I know how much: _____ ☐ Yes, but I don't know how much
☐ I need to research this   ☐ Definitely not

OTHER LOANS

☐ Yes and I know how much: _____ ☐ Yes, but I don't know how much
☐ I need to research this   ☐ Definitely not

part 2: who to ask?

Researching our resources can get complicated. Sometimes it includes an epic cast of family members and professionals, each with a different piece of the picture and with different responsibilities and concerns. Sometimes there's just one person wearing every single hat there is, from money manager to mom. Either way, figuring out who knows what can help you succeed in your research.

Here's more about some of the most common characters involved with managing wealth, especially if you are an inheritor. If your wealth comes from earnings, you may find that you're already playing a number of these roles for yourself.

The Initiator created stuff like trusts and accounts that may be in your name. If there are rules and clauses related to your finances, this person helped make them up. Even if the initiator doesn't currently have direct power over your finances (or is no longer alive), they may still be exerting influence over how the money is used.

The Trustee usually has a legal responsibility, as in the case of a trust fund officer, to oversee how money is distributed, invested and used. Trustees can be anyone from a paid advisor to an old family friend.

The Setter-Upper is often an attorney or other estate planner who helped the Initiator set things up. This is one person who definitely knows the inner-workings of things like partnerships and wills. They may also hold copies of the original documents (which can sometimes be surprisingly hard to come by).

The Guardian is a family member who had or has direct caretaking responsibility for you. They may have a range of control over your actual financial decisions, but no matter what they definitely have their opinion!

The Manager invests and manages assets and keeps track of income, profit and loss. This could be anyone from a representative at a large investment company to your aunt.

The Taxman prepares the taxes and may hold copies of past returns. Tax returns aren't necessarily the easiest thing to decode, but they can hold a ton of information.

The Recordkeeper keeps track of financial statements, investment reports and sometimes even legal documents. They often have a good sense of how everything fits together. This person may be a bookkeeper, an accountant, an office administrator or even a family member with a shoebox of old bank statements.

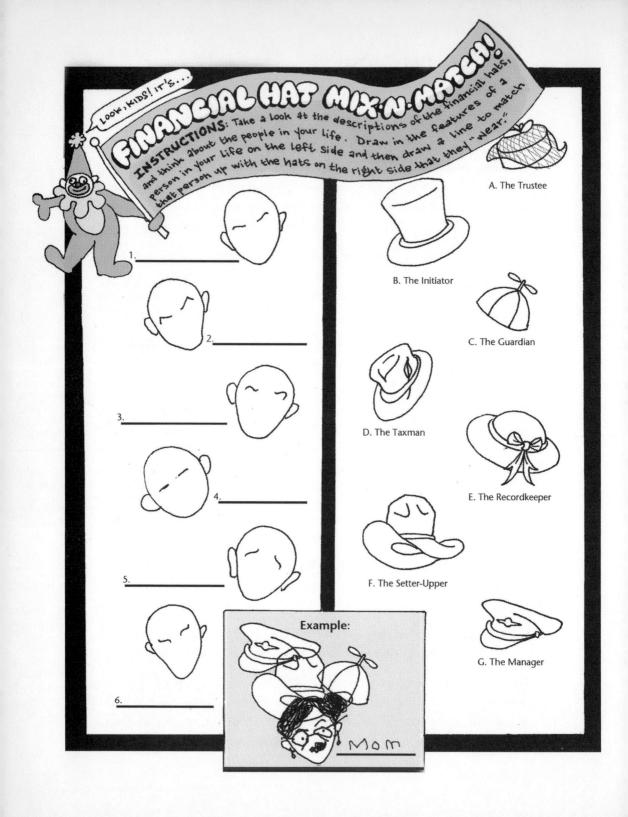

Look, KIDS! It's...

FINANCIAL HAT MIX·N·MATCH!

INSTRUCTIONS: Take a look at the descriptions of the financial hats, and think about the people in your life. Draw in the features of a person in your life on the left side and then draw a line to match that person up with the hats on the right side that they "wear."

A. The Trustee

B. The Initiator

C. The Guardian

D. The Taxman

E. The Recordkeeper

F. The Setter-Upper

G. The Manager

1. _____

2. _____

3. _____

4. _____

5. _____

6. _____

Example:

Mom _____

part 3: setting up a conversation

As you think about the roles different people are playing, it can also be useful to take a closer look at your relationships with them and how a potential conversation about your resources might go. The way you frame your questions and your goals can make a big difference.

▓ Do you feel comfortable approaching this person to have a conversation about money? If not, why not? Is there anything you can do to help make it easier for you? (Like having an ally with you, or setting the conversation on your own turf.)   .

▓ How would you describe your current relationship? How have issues around money and security played out in your relationship in the past? What can you do to help reframe the conversation and change past patterns?

▓ What values do you have in common? Where do you clash? Is it possible to focus the conversation around common ground or goals?

the using money for social change action plan

I'm making this plan because I believe...

What are some of my long-term goals for using money
for social change?

What's a doable scope for this plan? How can I use this plan to
help me move towards my long-term goals?

This plan is for the following year(s): _____

Currently I have approximately this much money:_____

Here are some of the tough questions I want to remember to keep
asking myself throughout the course of this plan:

I'm going evaluate and adjust my plan every _____ months.

Who needs to be a part of this planning process with me?

Who can I count on to be my support team throughout the course of this plan?

When I'm feeling discouraged, I should remember this because it always inspires me:

Would more financial education make it easier for me to put my plan into action? If yes, what steps am I going to take to build my financial skills?

investing/saving

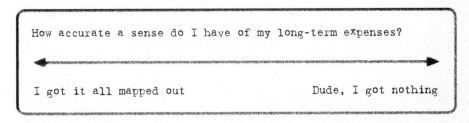

How accurate a sense do I have of my long-term expenses?

I got it all mapped out   Dude, I got nothing

I am going to keep $ _____ in investments and savings.

How close is this amount to what I estimate I will need for my long-term expenses?

What steps can I take to get a better sense of my long-term expenses?

My plan to make my current investments and savings more socially responsible is:

In order to get that done, what research do I need to do? Who should I talk to for advice or help?

Do I currently own any stocks? If so, what's my plan to research those companies I hold stock in? What's my plan to make my holdings more in line with my values or to get involved with shareholder activism?

Do I have control over how my assets are currently invested? If not, who do I need to talk to in order to get started on making them more socially responsible? What is my strategy for getting these decision-makers on board with my plan?

Start breaking down the tasks above into smaller action steps and create a timeline: (For example: I will find out how much life insurance costs by April 9.)

I will _____ by _____

I will _____ by _____

I will _____ by _____

I will _____ by _____

I will _____ by _____

earning

My goal is to earn $_____ a year.

How close am I currently to meeting this goal?

If I need to change my employment situation in order to meet this goal, what is my plan for doing so?

What kind of research do I need to do to put this plan into action? Who should I talk to for advice or help?

Start breaking down the tasks above into smaller action steps and create a timeline:

I will _____ by ____

I will _____ by ____

I will _____ by ____

I will _____ by ____

I will _____ by ____

spending

How close am I currently to having an accurate yearly budget?

← ─── →

I am the budget king!   Not close at all

My goal is to keep my expenses to $_____a year.

How realistic is that goal, based on my current budgeting experience?

What is my plan for monitoring my budget?

What's my plan for becoming a more responsible consumer?

What do I think about taxes? Should I be trying to pay more or less? What's my plan?

What kind of research do I need to do to put these plans into action? Who should I talk to for advice or help?

Start breaking down the tasks above into smaller action steps and create a timeline:

I will _____ by ___

I will _____ by ___

I will _____ by ___

I will _____ by ___

I will _____ by ___

giving

I will give a total of $_____ over the course of this plan.

I will complete my giving by the following date: _____.

My goal is to give away _____% of my _____ (assets or income).

Will my giving have a focus area? What's my plan for making this decision? Who am I going to make this decision with?

What's my plan for creating a more collaborative decision-making process (see the exercise in Chapter 11 for help on this):

What kind of research do I need to do to put this plan into action? Who should I talk to for advice or help?

Do I have control over all the assets I want to give? If not, who do I need to talk to in order to get started with my giving? What is my strategy for getting these decision-makers on board with my plan?

What's my plan for building better communication with the people I'm giving to?

What kind of giving goals have I set in the past? What made it possible for me to reach those goals or difficult to achieve them?

What did I learn that could help me reach my goals now?

Start breaking down the tasks above into smaller action steps and create a timeline:

I will _____ by _____

I will _____ by _____

I will _____ by _____

I will _____ by _____

I will _____ by _____

tips for sticking to an action plan

■ *Set a doable timeline*. Remember that all tasks are basically required to take longer than you think they will. When choosing deadlines, it helps to at least double your estimates of how long something will take, since it's a lot more encouraging to be ahead of schedule than to constantly feel behind.

■ *Break goals down* into smaller, more manageable action steps. Then break those steps down into even itty bittier pieces. Small = doable. Too big = overwhelming.

■ *Make dates with yourself*—actually write them in your calendar—once every week or two when you can put aside some time to work on the plan.

■ *Make a date to work on the plan together* with someone from your support team. Give yourself deadlines that must be completed before that time so you can report back to them. Don't forget to buy them a nice lunch while you're at it!

■ *Get a buddy:* team up with someone else who is working on their money action plan and support and nag each other.

■ Sometimes taking action is tangible. It's voting a shareholder proxy or writing a check. Sometimes it looks less concrete, like reading a book or making a call. Don't forget to *give yourself credit* for all the steps it takes to put your plan into action. In the end, it's the small, unglamorous stuff that'll get you there.

■ Sometimes the emotional part of this work can sneak up on us. When "call financial advisor" has been on the to-do list for two months but you just can't force yourself to do it, it's often the sign of a big ol' emotional block. This is when it's time to *step back and sort through all the feelings* a task brings up. Once you have a better understanding of what's up, it's easier to get back on track.

■ If you *make sticking to the plan a high priority*, it will absolutely get done, no matter what the challenges ahead. Put it low on the list, like after laundry and cleaning the bathroom, and it will never happen. This is about our values! About our hope for the world! About being true to ourselves! Don't wait—you can clean the shower tomorrow. Get started on your plan today!

■ Start *where you are*. If you wait until you feel prepared or until you know everything you think you need to know, then you'll never start at all.

■ If you're feeling nervous or overwhelmed by how much there is to do, try seeing if you can *start out by devoting an hour* to it a week—it's amazing how far you can get in just that short amount of time.

evaluating how things are going

Some simple questions to ask yourself to evaluate how the plan is going:

- Is this plan helping me align my resources with my values?

- Have I learned things lately that I should incorporate into the plan or that I should use to revise the plan?

- Do my goals still feel realistic?

- What strategies are working best and which ones aren't?

- Are there things in my plan that I've been avoiding? How come?

- Am I asking my support team for help when I need it? Do I feel like I'm getting the support I need to help me stick to the plan?

- Am I challenging myself to do things that make me uncomfortable or afraid? What have I learned from this?

- Am I putting my social change values into practice not only in the actions I'm taking, but in my process? How's it going?

- What's one thing I've done so far that feels like a big success?

- What's something I want to do differently next time?

156

SAM

WHY IS THIS SO HARD TO FIGURE OUT?

I'VE ALWAYS GOTTEN STRAIGHT A'S IN MATH — SO WHY IS IT THAT WHENEVER I LOOK AT A FINANCIAL STATEMENT, MY BRAIN TURNS TO MUSH AND ALL THE NUMBERS START SWIMMING AROUND ON THE PAGE?

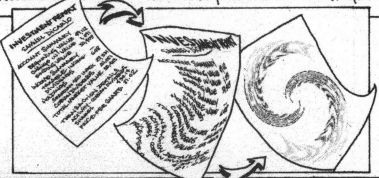

MY DAD DIED A YEAR AGO. HE HAD A HEART ATTACK, AND BOOM.

IT WAS PRETTY SURREAL — GUYS IN SUITS SHOWED UP TO HIS FUNERAL WITH PAPERS FOR ME AND MY SISTER TO SIGN.

MY FOLKS HAD BEEN DIVORCED FOR LIKE 20 YEARS; THEY WEREN'T EVEN SPEAKING. SO ALL THE MONEY WENT STRAIGHT TO MY SISTER & ME, 50-50.

I DON'T KNOW WHAT I PICTURED EXACTLY — THAT SOME GUY WOULD SHOW UP ON MY DOORSTEP AND HAND ME ONE OF THOSE BIG CHECKS LIKE THEY DO ON TV?

SAM DICARLO $150,000 CONGRATULATIONS!

YAY! WOO-HOO!!

APPLAUSE! APPLAUSE!

BUT ALL THAT HAPPENED WAS MY DAD'S ACCOUNTS GOT QUIETLY, UNCERE-MONIOUSLY TRANSFERRED TO MY NAME....

AND I STARTED GETTING A LOT MORE MAIL.

CHAPTER 13

Using Privilege for Social Change

In the first half of this book, we spent a lot of time looking at how having wealth is about much more than money. It's about the connections we have to other wealthy people and the networks that are open to us. It's about the access we have to institutions and to those who run them. Even with an empty bank account, we can still be carting some pretty intense class privilege. Now that we've broken down all its ins and outs, it's time to put this privilege to work for social change.

The strategies in this chapter can get a bit more complicated than the ones in Chapters 10 and 11. This is because access and connections, while extremely powerful, aren't tangible like cash. We can't transfer them or give them away or even stack them up in little piles in a briefcase. Most of these strategies require some serious labor, lots of communication and long-term temerity. But if we can pull them off, they're also some of the most effective social change work we can do as people with privilege.

strategy #1: building a dialogue about social change with people with wealth

It's hard to talk with someone about social change giving or investing if they don't know what you mean by social change. We don't have to win them over to an entire world-view, just build enough common understanding to start a conversation. Proving that social change is a valid topic for debate (and that we aren't raving lunatics) can sometimes be a giant step in itself. This can take time, so start slow.

Here are a few ideas for getting a dialogue going:

■ Try starting the conversation off *by asking about something they're passionately involved in.* What makes it meaningful to them? Even if they're only describing stamp collecting, as long as it inspires them to action—they did join that National Duck Stamp Collectors Society, after all—you can use this to segue into a dialogue about values and community.

■ Try *sharing reading materials.* Just make sure it's something you're reading too. You want it to feel like you're lending a favorite book instead of being The Teacher.

■ *Plan an outing together.* Go to an event, a fundraising party, a community meeting, a protest, or a talk—anything that's exciting and will let them see with their own eyes what you're talking about.

■ *Do something arty* that deals with social change themes. Watch a video, go to a movie, a concert, an exhibit or a play. Just make sure you know your audience and don't rush it. You'll probably want to wait a bit before you hit that anarchist-collective's body-painting exhibition.

strategy #2: inspiring people with wealth to give more money to social change

In general, the trick here is to be inspiring and get people excited versus making them feel stressed, guilty or like you're taking advantage of them. This isn't always easy to do because sometimes just bringing up the topic of giving can make people with wealth really uncomfortable. Keep in mind that different situations call for different styles: sometimes you'll need to slowly build up to a conversation about giving in general, sometimes you can jump right in and fundraise. Here are a few tried and true ways to start the dialogue:

■ Open up the topic by *talking about your own giving*. It doesn't matter if you only give a small amount, it's the fact that you've taken action that will inspire people. Plus, they will feel more like you're asking them to join your cool giving team instead of telling them what they should do.

■ *Make a holiday gift donation in their name.* If it's hard to bring up the topic of giving, this is a way to at least introduce an organization you're trying to help fundraise for. Be careful to make the gift in a generous spirit, in a way that says, "Here's something I am excited about. I made this contribution in your honor." As opposed to, "I am trying to balance out the evil you do in the world by making this donation in your name."

■ *Share your activism.* Even if they're not that interested in the issues you're involved with, friends and family are often still interested in you and want to support what-ever you're doing. For this to work, it's important that you're truly sharing a part of your life. Try bringing a flyer from a recent event or pictures of you at a rally.

■ If you're planning to outright fundraise and pitch a donation to a specific orga-nization, you should always give people a heads-up before-hand. No one likes a fundraising sneak attack. (A simple, "Can I tell you about this group I'm trying to raise money for?" will do it.) Once you have their okay, *come prepared.* Think ahead about what kinds of questions they might ask and how you'll answer them. Bring along lots of materials like brochures, annual reports and budgets.

strategy #3: inspiring people with wealth to make their investments more socially responsible

■ *Sharing your own financial planning decisions* is always a good conversation opener. Even if you just have a checking account at a community development bank or you buy your groceries at the local co-op, it shows that you put your money where your mouth is.

■ *Be aware of the language you use.* While "socially responsible investing" is a standard name for this stuff, it can make some people feel judged, as if you are saying that they are personally irresponsible. You want to be sharing options with them, not making them feel like you think they are an evil, uncaring pighead.

■ *Be ready with the literature and articles.* Most people's biggest resistance to socially responsible investing is that they feel it doesn't make a profit or that it is some hippy dippy thing instead of an actual investment strategy. This is the perfect time to say something like, "I read this great book that's all about that..."

■ Here's a slightly undercover way to begin a conversation with the more conservative, business people types in your life: *ask them to explain something to you.* For example, if you ask about how proxies work or what shareholder responsibility means, you can end up moving the discussion towards shareholder activism. The advantage of this strategy is that it shows you respect their opinion, which is always the right foot to start out on.

strategy #4: challenging people with wealth when they're acting out Side Effects

We've all done it. Sometimes we assume that everyone around us has the same resources and options that we do. Or we end up doing one of the class privilege Side Effects and acting like being wealthy means our needs are more important than anyone else's or that we should always be in charge.

While we're doing our best to keep an eye on our own actions, we also need to be willing to challenge each other. We can't stay silent when we see other people with wealth acting on class privilege assumptions.

Right about now you might be thinking, "Sure, that's a nice idea in theory. But does it actually work? Does it even make a difference?" Honestly, it really does. Challenging each other isn't easy: sometimes it's life-changing for everyone involved, sometimes the whole process tanks. It takes practice. Still, because we come from similar experiences with privilege, we can challenge each other in some very powerful ways. In fact, this is one of the most effective strategies for using our privilege for social change.

But how can we challenge someone without coming off like a grandstanding jerk? Here are a few tips:

- *The last thing you want is to sound judgmental.* Let them know you've done the same thing yourself. Even if you haven't done the exact same thing, you can probably think of something close enough.

- Try to *speak from a place of compassion and empathy*, not anger. Of course, this is definitely easier said than done! Practice helps. (Check out the Resource Section for organizations that do trainings in communication and anti-oppression education.)

- In most group situations it's best to pull a person aside and have a private conversation with them so they don't feel embarrassed in front of others. However, if someone is disrespecting or attacking another person in the group, it can be important to say something in the moment. As people with privilege, *it's crucial for us to challenge each other* instead of expecting those who are being attacked to do the challenging for us.

- It makes a big difference if you can have *a positive interaction with the person not too long after* the whole challenge thing goes down. You want to let them know that you're their ally in figuring this stuff out, and that being in an on-going relationship is important to you.

- Understanding privilege is a long and complicated process and you can't force people to get on board if they don't want to. Still, it's possible that something you say now may stick with someone and inspire them later on. *So don't give up hope…*

Sometimes this strategy for challenging people works well. You have a great conversation and the other person is so glad you pointed it out because they didn't even know they were doing it. Sometimes it's a tense but civil discussion where it's clear that the other person thinks you're pretentious and annoying.

And sometimes, no matter how hard we try, all hell breaks loose. At moments like these it can help to remember a few things:

- *Keep calm.* Don't forget to breathe. Do your best to stay with the conversation and be patient. If they are attacking you, try not to take it personally.

- *Don't make assumptions* about what's going on for them. Just listen.

- *Pay attention to your body language.* You want to show that you're open to keeping the dialogue going instead of closing it off. Watch out for guarded or frustrated body language, like hunching inwards, folding your arms, squinting or frowning.

Finally, here are a few examples of when to use this strategy:

- Whenever the wealthier people in a group assume that everyone has the same privileged options as they do. This can take the form of assuming everyone has access to a car, can afford to take time off, can put something on a credit card, can afford to go to a pricier restaurant or chip in for expenses. Or when they don't realize that some members of the group may need help with things like childcare or transportation in order to participate.

- When people's opinions are being disparaged at work or school solely because they have a lower salary or position.

- A chance to challenge the assumption that a person's worth is only equal to how much money they have is probably coming up if you hear a phrase like: good stock, well-bred, gold digger, red neck, well-heeled, white trash, down and out, first class, social climber, welfare queen, upstanding, bum.

- Any time someone tells a more conventional money story like, "He worked his way up to the top from nothing, all on his own," or, "Through smart investing, she grew a small fortune." This is a good opportunity to put your own revised money story to use.

- Whenever someone working in a service job is being treated with disrespect.

strategy #5: learning how to challenge other forms of discrimination

Class privilege assumptions can often come bundled together with other kinds of discrimination like racism, sexism and homophobia. It's essential that we educate ourselves about the many different shapes privilege can take and that we learn how to speak out against oppression in *all* its forms. The more we learn, the more effective we will be in all of our social change work. There are some amazing workshops, trainings and books out there—see the list in the Resource Section for some ideas on where to begin.

strategy #6: building communication skills

The better we are at communicating, the better all of these strategies will work. If we're always acting holier-than-thou or we stink at listening respectfully, our dialogues will all end in frustration. A few techniques that can help:

- If you've never talked with someone about wealth, privilege or social change before, *don't just jump in and start a conversation on impulse.* Spend some time thinking about it beforehand. What can you say that will be meaningful and moving to them?

- *Have realistic goals* for the dialogues you are opening up. In general, it's better to move slowly and get a sense of how a person feels about the conversation than to push too hard and have to backtrack.

- *Pay attention to atmosphere:* where are you planning on having the conversation? Try and choose somewhere the other person feels comfortable. And don't forget snacks—low blood sugar is the enemy of social change.

- *Pick a good time:* don't start a big conversation about social change when someone is feeling exhausted, overwhelmed or anxious. If you're meeting up for a meal or for coffee, make sure neither of you are going to be in a rush to get to another appointment.

- *Getting some training* is always a good idea—check out the Resource Section for ideas.

- *Pay attention to what vocabulary a person uses* for things like wealth, privilege and social change. Then adjust your own terminology. This can make the difference between a conversation that feels like an exchange of ideas versus one that feels like an intimidating lecture.

strategy #7: connecting with other young people with wealth who believe in social change

There are a lot of us out there. We've got to start talking to each other! Challenging each other! Inspiring each other! One rich kid using their privilege for social change is great. One hundred? That's better. One hundred thousand? *Now* we're talking...

Finding other young people with wealth isn't always easy since so many of us keep our class privilege hidden. The main way to do it is to be as open as we can about our own privilege and values, and then let them find us. There's a whole range of ways to make this happen, from low-key to pretty bold, depending on what you're up for:

- *Having more open conversations about our privilege* is the simplest way to find other rich kids. Sometimes it turns out that the person we're talking with has class privilege, too, and has been waiting all their lives to be able to talk about it with someone else who knows what it's like. Or the person we're talking to will pass our name on to a wealthy friend who's been keeping their privilege hidden. No matter what the outcome, we're opening up more honest dialogue about class and privilege, which is always a good thing. WARNING: watch out for pushing too hard—if the subject comes up, cool. If the other person is interested in talking more about class, great. Don't force it. ("Hey, that's good salsa! Did I mention that I have class privilege?")

- Know anyone who works with wealthy people as part of their jobs? Like financial or philanthropic professionals? Tell them you'd be psyched to *serve as a resource for any of their younger clients* who might be feeling isolated. You could also give them a stack of relevant books to pass on to any young people with wealth they know.

- *Have you ever gone to school with a lot of other wealthy kids?* If you're there right now, then just start looking around you! If you've already graduated, remember that alum events are a good way to reconnect and find out if anyone there fits the social change profile. What about teachers you know—do any of them look at social justice issues as part of their curriculum? You might be able to help them introduce questions of privilege into the classroom by offering to talk about your experiences. You can also try donating relevant books to the library and making sure the counseling office has resources available.

- There are usually at least a few other young people with wealth who believe in social change at most *philanthropy conferences and fundraising events.* And since giving is already the topic of the day, it can be a little easier to start up a conversation.

- Here's an obvious one: *go to a conference or workshop specifically for people with wealth.* RG keeps a calendar of these events at www.resourcegeneration.org.

- If you're feeling bold, what about *writing an article for a school paper or alumni magazine?* The more publicly you put yourself out there, the easier it is for other young people with wealth to find you.

strategy #8: getting together

If you do meet another young person with wealth who believes in social change, try making plans to get together and keep the conversation going. That's when all the good supporting and challenging each other stuff can happen. Besides, this work is hard, and the more buddies we have going through the same thing, the better.

At a loss for what to talk about? Here are a few questions that can help break the ice:

- What's your vision of social change? How have your experiences with wealth influenced your vision?

- Where does your wealth/the wealth in your family come from?

- Do you feel like having wealth has ever affected your relationships? Do you ever talk about it with the people in your life? What have those conversations been like?

Another powerful way we can inspire and challenge each other is by sharing stories about our experiences with privilege. A few ideas:

- Share your alternate money story and what it was like to research that. (See Chapter 7.)

- Talk about what it means to you to be working towards social change as a young person with wealth. What inspires you? What's been a challenge? (See the "Social Change Star" exercise in Chapter 2.)

- Talk about some of the ways having class privilege has impacted your life. (See Chapter 4.)

- Talk about your own process of coming to terms with your class privilege. What has it been like? How has it changed the way you see things and the way you take action for social change?

And here are a few storytelling tips:

■ A couple of interesting details always make a story come alive. *(For example: This happened around the time my dad got that mullet...)*

■ Try to be specific about how you felt and what your process was like. Avoid saying vague things like, "It was a big deal for me." Tell them *why*.

■ Don't be afraid to talk about moments that were deeply emotional for you. These are often the most meaningful stories you can tell.

Finally, part of the point of getting together is to make sure that people know they don't have to do this work alone. And in fact, we're all going to be a lot more effective if we're linked into some larger organizations that will support and challenge us. So don't forget to hook them up with groups like RG that have programs for young people with wealth, and with books and other resources that might be helpful.

strategy #9: collaborating with social change groups

When social change groups plan strategy, brainstorming together about who knows who is an important step. It's a way to figure out how each person involved can use their connections to move the group closer to its goals. This is also one of those times where, as young people with wealth in the room, we often remain silent about our access and connections. In that moment, even doing a naked version of the Macarena can seem like a less embarrassing and isolating option than talking about our privilege. And sharing that information in front of a whole group *is* scary, at least at the beginning. But imagine how much more effective we could be if we'd all just jump in and start collaborating! Besides, everyone would be teasing us about that naked Macarena thing for the rest of our lives...

This strategy can take many different forms, depending on the kinds of access we have and the issues we're involved with. Even if our networks aren't relevant to the problem at hand, we can still put those connections to work through fundraising. Here are a few examples of what this strategy looks like in action:

■ Bringing a key decision-maker to the table for a meeting or negotiation.

■ Enlisting the support of a local leader for a campaign.

■ Helping place an article about the group's work into the media.

- Helping fundraise.

- Introducing group leaders to donors.

- Helping to bring out the support of a university's students and professors.

- Representing the group's views at a restricted-access meeting—or figuring out how to get everyone else through the door with you.

It's important to keep in mind that this strategy only succeeds when we're working as part of a larger group and making these decisions together as a cross-class team. This is one of those moments where the process really is as important as the action itself. If we don't collaborate on how to use our access and connections, we're actually putting a bunch of the Side Effects into play: we're assuming that because we have privilege, we automatically know what's right for the group and what will be most effective for social change. Without a collaborative process, we can end up undermining our own best intentions.

"I think coming together and talking about how to use our resources is really important. But I think it's actually kind of dangerous to stop there. Coming together with people who have similar class backgrounds is crucial, but it's crucial so that we can then be in cross-class circles and work to create real change together."—Nicole

"Where I belong taking leadership is with other rich white people. That's a really hard thing for me to do because every atom in my body wants to run the other way and surround myself only with people of color and working class people. But that's not a place for me to be taking leadership. Anytime I start feeling the need to liberate people of color or working class people, it's a red flag that there's something I need to work on in myself.

I always feel like I'm actively upholding the same system of inequality that I'm trying to fight against. It feels like my background can't coexist with my politics, that one's got to go and I'm not willing to give up my values.

But then I'm not tapping into circles that I have access to. I end up protesting outside buildings when I could be inside sitting at the table. I end up feeling like I'm raging against myself because the two sides are so polarized that they're at war with each other. It's much scarier to demand that the two parts of me have a voice and work together. But that's what needs to happen for anything to change."—Molly

CHAPTER 14

Creating a Privilege Action Plan

N ow comes the real thrill—mapping out how we're going to put all these strategies into action! For tips on sticking to an action plan and evaluating how things are going, see the end of Chapter 12.

brainstorming connections

Many of the strategies in the last two chapters require building on our connections to other people with wealth and those who work as their advisors. So it's worth spending some time figuring out who we know and how those connections can fit into our action plans.

A quick warning: sometimes doing this exercise can feel depressing because it lists only the people *with wealth* we know. It doesn't reflect all the other people who are a part of our lives. Just remember that this isn't meant to be a map of our relationships or of those who are closest to our hearts. It's only meant to be a list of the personal connections we have to people with wealth because of our class privilege.

To get started, ask:

■ Who do I know that's a person with wealth?

■ Who do I know that advises people with wealth?

Then for each person on your list, think about questions like:

■ What kind of relationship do we currently have?

■ What kind of institutional access or decision-making power do they have?

■ What kind of influence do they have over current laws or policies?
   Over public opinion?

■ Are they interested in social change? In giving or philanthropy?

Here's a list of places that can help you brainstorm about the people with wealth you might know:

People you know from...

■ Your family

■ Your neighborhood

■ Your job

■ Family friends

■ Religious institutions

- Cultural groups or organizations
- Exclusive membership groups like country clubs or museum associations
- Volunteer and charity groups
- Non-profit boards

Finance and law

- Financial professionals like brokers, accountants, advisors or planners
- Banking professionals
- Investment managers
- Lawyers, especially those who specialize in estate planning

Philanthropy

- People at foundations or funds
- People from philanthropic membership organizations or conferences
- Philanthropy professionals like advisors or fundraisers

Schools

- Fellow students and alumni
- Student group leaders
- Professors, deans, counselors
- Fraternity/sorority members or other club members

Government and business

- Government and elected officials
- Corporate leaders
- Small business leaders
- People from business or industry associations

Arts and media

- Media producers and editors
- Famous or influential artists, musicians, writers, actors, directors...

thinking about ethics

No matter how dedicated we are to using our privilege for social change, there will always be some thorny ethical issues surrounding the whole endeavor.

While money is moveable, class privilege isn't something we can give away, share or transfer. It remains grounded in our own body, which means it's often still working for our benefit even while we're trying to use it towards different ends. And while a dollar bill has no particular mission other than to circulate, class privilege has a purpose: to keep the unjust distribution of resources in place. Trying to use our privilege for change goes against its very design specifications, which can make for a particularly rocky road.

That's why it's important that we incorporate questions of ethics into our plans and then constantly revisit them as we put those plans into action.

Here are a few of the big ethics questions we've struggled with at RG again and again:

■ What's the difference between using our privilege to support and fundraise for something we are directly involved in versus something we are not directly involved in? What about the difference between using it to support something we started or that we lead versus something run by others?

■ Where is the line between trying to build our access and connections so that we can use them for social change and trying to build them for our own benefit? What about if we're building them for social change and benefiting at the same time?

■ Where is the line between building our access and power in an institution in order to be able to challenge it more effectively and just building our own career and prestige?

■ Where's the line between spending lots of time with wealthy people as part of our social change work and spending lots of time with wealthy people because we feel more comfortable with them?

■ Where's the line between spending lots of time working together for social change with people who have less privilege than we do and avoiding working together for social change with wealthy people?

■ How can we share our contacts with wealthy people in a way that is respectful? How can we make sure that the wealthy people we know feel cared for and not exploited?

■ How can we make sure that the people we are collaborating with are able to build their own relationships with our connections instead of always having to go through us?

■ Are there people in our lives who challenge us on these questions? If there aren't, are we purposefully sheltering ourselves from having more challenging relationships?

the using privilege for social change action plan

I'm making this plan because I believe...

This plan is for the following year(s): _____

Here are some of the big ethical questions that I intend to keep asking throughout the course of this plan:

I'm going to evaluate how things are going with my plan every _____ months.

I can count on these people to be my support team throughout the course of this plan:

When I'm feeling discouraged, I should remember this because it always inspires me:

What trainings, workshops or readings should I check out to help build my understanding of privilege and discrimination?

What trainings, workshops or readings should I check out to help build my communication skills?

building dialogue

Some of the people with wealth I want to start building a dialogue with are:

What's my plan for doing this?

What are some realistic goals for these dialogues, both long-term and short-term?

What do I need to do to prepare for starting up these conversations? Is there research I need to do? Who should I talk to for advice or help?

Are there current situations in which I've noticed other people with wealth acting out class privilege Side Effects? What's my plan for saying something next time I see the situation occur?

What's my plan for putting myself out there so other young people with wealth can find me?

My goal is to meet at least _____ young people with wealth who believe in social change this year, and to get together to talk more
with at least ___ of them.

Start breaking down the tasks above into smaller action steps and
create a timeline: (For example: I will <u>have a conversation with</u>
<u>Fred</u> by <u>September 12.</u>)

I will _____ by _____

I will _____ by _____

I will _____ by _____

I will _____ by _____

I will _____ by _____

building on connections

What are some of the ways I could build on my connections to help
support social change groups?

Are there connections I have that could be helpful to a particular movement or group that I'm already working with? If so,
what's my plan for sharing this info with them and building a
strategy together?

Are there connections I have that could be helpful to a particular movement or group that I'm not currently involved with? If so,
what's my plan for getting more involved? (See the "Research Tips"
exercise at the end of Chapter 11 for some ideas.)

What kind of relationship do I have with my "connections"? Am
I ready to start working with them towards a specific social
change goal? What's my plan for opening up a conversation about
this with them?

What do I need to do to prepare for taking any of these actions?
Is there research I need to do? Who should I talk to for advice
or help?

Start breaking down the tasks above into smaller action steps
and create a timeline:

I will _____ by _____

I will _____ by _____

I will _____ by _____

I will _____ by _____

I will _____ by _____

CHAPTER

What's Next?

ou made it! This is the end! Unless of course you're reading the book backwards, and then this is just the beginning. Either way, working to understand our class privilege and using it to support social change is a lifelong endeavor, so there's plenty more road up ahead for all of us. This is a good time to remember to pace yourself, because we all need to be able to stick with this work for the long run.

With all the options, exercises and plans in this book, the question of *what's next* can feel a bit overwhelming. Where should we start? What's the right way to do it? Thankfully, there is no one right way. We each have to find our own path. And the only place to start is wherever we are right now. It's a "put one foot in front of the other and walk" kind of thing—even if we haven't entirely figured out where we're going yet.

The only certainty in all this is that it's going to be a very different journey than the one class privilege prepares us for. In the world of class privilege, success means approval and tangible achievements. It's measurable through prestige, degrees, awards and bank accounts. Challenging the unjust distribution of resources, however, is *definitely* not on the list of approved things to do with our privilege. So our success is bound to look quite different.

Success may mean hitting resistance. As activist Linda Stout says, "If we are not getting opposition, then we must not be doing enough!" It may mean that some people will look at us like we're weird or even crazy. It may mean making deep changes and even sacrifices in our lives—since if there truly is going to be a more just distribution of resources, it's going to necessitate letting go of some of our own wealth and losing some of our privilege.

Most of all, success will mean waking up each morning knowing that we are putting our values into action. That we are living a life that's in line with our belief in social change. That we were brave enough to look head-on at some of the injustice in the world and to see how our own privilege played a part in keeping it going. And that we did not choose to turn away, but instead took a stand.

Resource Section

selected sources

Some of the writing that had a big influence on this book...

James Baldwin, *The Price of the Ticket: Collected Nonfiction 1948-1985*,
St. Martins, 1985.

"To do your first works over means to reexamine everything. Go back to where you
started, or as far back as you can, examine all of it, travel your road again and tell
the truth about it. Sing or shout or testify or keep it to yourself: *but know whence you
came.* This is precisely what the generality of white Americans cannot afford to do."

Paulo Freire, *Pedagogy of the Oppressed*, Continuum, 1997.

"In order to have the continued opportunity to express their 'generosity,' the
oppressors must perpetuate injustice as well. An unjust social order is the permanent fount of this 'generosity'.... True generosity consists precisely in fighting to
destroy the causes which nourish false charity.... This lesson and this apprentice-
ship must come, however, from the oppressed themselves and from those who are
truly solidary with them."

bell hooks, *Where We Stand: Class Matters*, Routledge, 2000.

"To be wealthy and remain committed to justice is no easy task. We hear little from
the wealthy who use their means to further the cause of justice, of economic self-
sufficiency for all. Despite their good deeds, this silence maintains their class solidar-
ity with those who exploit and oppress, as they are best situated to challenge their
peers, to offer new ways of thinking and being in the world."

James W. Loewen, *Lies My Teacher Told Me: Everything Your American History Textbook
Got Wrong*, Touchstone, 1995.

"Thinking well of education reinforces the ideology we might call American indi-
vidualism. It leaves intact the archetypal image of a society marked by or at least
striving toward equality of opportunity. Yet precisely to the extent that students
believe that equality of opportunity exists, they are encouraged to blame the
uneducated for being poor.... Americans who are not poor find American individu-
alism a satisfying ideology, for it explains their success in life by laying it at their
own doorstep.... It is much more gratifying to believe that their educational attain-
ments and occupational successes result from ambition and hard work—that their
privilege has been earned."

Audre Lorde, *Sister Outsider: Essays and Speeches,* Crossing Press, 1984.

"The master's tools will never dismantle the master's house. They may allow us temporarily to beat him at his own game, but they will never enable us to bring about genuine change. And this fact is only threatening to those women who still define the master's house as their only source of support."

Thomas M. Shapiro, *The Hidden Cost of Being African American: How Wealth Perpetuates Inequality,* Oxford University Press, 2004.

"We can no longer ignore tremendous wealth inequalities as we struggle with the thorny issue of racial inequality. Without attending to how equal opportunity or even equal achievement does not lead to equal results—especially concerning wealth—we will continue to repeat the deep and disturbing patterns of racial inequality and conflict that plague our republic."

resources

This is *so* not a complete list. Like the book, it's limited to stuff in the U.S. and focuses mainly on class privilege and economic justice. There's a tiny bit of other stuff in there, too, but hopefully this is just snack on the way to a big ol' main course of research.

A few great resource lists that are a lot more complete than this one are available at: www.classism.org, www.faireconomy.org, www.thepeoplesinstitute.org, www.classmatters.org and www.coopamerica.org.

By the way, whenever there's a blurb about an organization, it's usually just pulled out of their mission statement. (Organizations whose names give you an idea of what they do don't have blurbs.) And all book information corresponds to the most current available edition.

how to get in touch with resource generation

www.resourcegeneration.org
(617) 225-3939

other organizations that work specifically with people with wealth

Inheritance Project

www.inheritance-project.com

Provides educational resources and support for inheritors of wealth and their families. They publish resources like *The Legacy of Inherited Wealth: Interviews with Heirs* that you can order on their website.

More than Money

www.morethanmoney.org
(617) 864-8200

Helps individuals step back and consider how their individual economic activity aligns with their most deeply held values. They also publish a quarterly journal.

Resourceful Women

www.rw.org
(415) 956-3023

Offers an array of classes, support groups and conferences for women who have $25,000 or more of inherited or earned money, to provide personal supports, technical assistance and an empowerment perspective.

a starter list of books for reading more about class

(Also see Selected Sources)

Dorothy Allison, *Skin: Talking about Sex, Class and Literature*, Firebrand Books, 2005.

Gloria E. Anzaldua and Analouise Keating, *This Bridge We Call Home: Radical Visions for Transformation*, Routledge, 2002.

Stanley Aronowitz, *How Class Works: Power and Social Movement*, Yale University Press, 2003.

Chuck Collins, Amy Gluckman, Betsy Leondar-Wright and others (eds.), *The Wealth Inequality Reader,* Dollars & Sense, 2004.

Chuck Collins and William H. Gates, *Wealth and Our Commonwealth: Why America Should Tax Accumulated Fortunes*, Beacon Press, 2004.

Ellis Cose, *The Rage of a Privileged Class: Why Do Prosperous Blacks Still Have the Blues?*, Perennial, 1995.

Angela Davis, *Women, Race and Class,* Vintage, 1983.

Diane Dujon and Ann Withhorn, *For Crying Out Loud: Women's Poverty in the United States*, South End Press, 1996.

Barbara Ehrenreich, *Nickel and Dimed: On (Not) Getting by in America,* Owl Books, 2002.

David Cay Johnston, *Perfectly Legal: The Covert Campaign to Rig Our Tax System to Benefit the Super Rich—and Cheat Everybody Else*, Portfolio, 2003.

Paul Kivel, *You Call This a Democracy?*, Apex Press, 2004.

Albert Lubrano, *Limbo: Blue-Collar Roots, White-Collar Dreams*, John Wiley and Sons, 2005.

Alice Lynd and Staughton Lynd (eds.), *The New Rank and File*, ILR Press, 2000.

Annalee Newitz and Matt Wray (eds.), *White Trash: Race and Class in America*, Routledge, 1996.

Gwendolyn M. Parker, *Trespassing: My Sojourn in the Halls of Privilege*, Mariner Books, 1999.

Susan Raffo (ed.), *Queerly Classed*, South End Press, 1997.

Holly Sklar, *Chaos or Community? Seeking Solutions, Not Scapegoats for Bad Economics*, South End Press, 1995.

Michelle Tea, *Without A Net: The Female Experience of Growing Up Working Class*, Seal Press, 2004.

Studs Turkel, *Working: People Talk About What They Do All Day and How They Feel About What They Do*, New Press, 1997.

Wimsatt, William Upski, *No More Prisons*, Subway and Elevated/Soft Skull Press, 1999.

Michael Zweig (ed.), *What's Class Got to Do With It?: American Society in the Twenty-First Century*, ILR Press, 2004.

economic justice organizations

50 Years is Enough: U.S. Network for Global Economic Justice
www.50years.org
(202) 463-2265
A U.S.-based coalition of over 200 organizations dedicated to the profound transformation of the World Bank and the International Monetary Fund.

Center for Economic Justice
www.econjustice.net
(505) 232-3100
Strengthens international movements that counter corporate-driven globalization and promote more just policy alternatives.

Fair Taxes for All Coalition
www.fairtaxes4all.org
A coalition committed to promoting a fair tax system that raises sufficient revenues to meet our shared priorities and invest in our common future.

Living Wage Resource Center
www.livingwagecampaign.org
(617) 740-9500
Info about the living wage movement and current living wage campaigns across the country.

Poor People's Economic Human Right's Campaign
www.economichumanrights.org
(888) 233-1948
Committed to uniting the poor across color lines as the leadership base for a broad movement to abolish poverty.

Responsible Wealth
www.responsiblewealth.org
(617) 423-2148
A national network of businesspeople, investors and affluent Americans who are concerned about deepening economic inequality and are working for wide-spread prosperity.

United for a Fair Economy (UFE)
www.faireconomy.org
(617) 423-2148
Raises awareness that concentrated wealth and power undermine the economy, corrupt democracy, deepen the racial divide and tear communities apart.

racial wealth gap

The Racial Wealth Divide Project
www.racialwealthdivide.org
(617) 423-2148, ext.17
Offers resources, workshops and publications.

Chuck Collins and Felice Yeskel, *Economic Apartheid in America: A Primer on Economic Inequality and Security*, New Press, 2000.

Melvin L. Oliver and Thomas M. Shapiro, *Black Wealth, White Wealth: A New Perspective on Racial Inequality*, Routledge, 1997.

Randall Robinson, *The Debt: What America Owes Blacks*, Dutton, 2000.

economics 101

The Center for Popular Economics
www.populareconomics.org
(413) 545-0743
A non-profit collective of political economists whose programs and publications demystify the economy and put useful economic tools in the hands of people fighting for social and economic justice.

Dollars and Sense
www.dollarsandsense.org
A bi-monthly magazine that offers an alternative look at the
economy with a vision for economic equity and justice.

Randy Charles Epping, *A Beginner's Guide to the World Economy,* Vintage, 2001.

Nancy Folbre, James Heintz, and the Center for Popular Economics, *The Ultimate Field Guide to the U.S. Economy,* New Press, 2000.

Robert L. Heilbroner, *The Worldly Philosophers: The Lives, Times And Ideas Of The Great Economic Thinkers,* Touchstone, 1999.

Amartya Sen, *Development as Freedom,* Anchor, 2000.

Joseph E. Stiglitz, *Globalization and Its Discontents,* W. W. Norton and Company, 2003.

cross class collaboration

Betsy Leondar-Wright, *Class Matters: Cross-Class Alliance Building for Middle-Class Activists,* New Society Publishers, 2005.
And for more resources see the companion website www.classmatters.org.

Fred Rose, *Coalitions across the Class Divide,* Cornell University, 2000.

Linda Stout, *Bridging the Class Divide and Other Lessons from Grassroots Organizing,* Beacon Press, 1997.

understanding privilege and oppression

Maurianne Adams, Warren J. Blumenfeld, Rosie Castaneda and others (eds.), *Readings for Diversity and Social Justice: An Anthology on Racism, Sexism, Anti-Semitism, Heterosexism, Classism, and Ableism,* Falmer Press, 2000.

Eduardo Bonilla-Silva, *Racism Without Racists,* Rowman & Littlefield Publishers, 2003

Kate Bornstein, *My Gender Workbook,* Routledge, 1998.

Karen Brodkin, *How Jews Became White Folks and What That Says About Race in America,* Rutgers University Press, 1999.

Dee Brown, *Bury My Heart at Wounded Knee: The Indian History of the American West,* Henry Holt & Company, 2001.

Daisy Hernandez and Bushra Rehman (eds.), *Colonize This!: Young Women of Color on Today's Feminism,* Seal Press, 2002.

Noel Ignatiev, *How the Irish Became White,* Routledge, 1996.

Allan G. Johnson, *Privilege, Power, and Difference,* McGraw Hill, 2001.

Amy Sonnie (ed.), *Revolutionary Voices: A Multicultural Queer Youth Anthology,* Alyson Publications, 2000.

Tim Wise, *White Like Me,* Soft Skull Press, 2005.

Frank H. Wu, *Yellow: Race in America Beyond Black and White,* Basic Books, 2001.

Howard Zinn, *A People's History of the United States: 1492–Present,* Perennial Classics, 2003.

anti-oppression education and training

Applied Resource Center
www.arc.org
(510) 653-3415
A public policy, educational and research institute whose work emphasizes issues of race and social change. They also publish *Colorlines Magazine,* the nation's leading magazine on race, culture and organizing.

Class Action
www.classism.org
(413) 585-9709
Class Action focuses on the personal, interpersonal and organizational levels of classism. They serve as a national resource center on class, providing individuals and organizations with the tools and resources to work on eliminating classism.

Challenging White Supremacy Workshop
www.cwsworkshop.org
(415) 647-0921
Committed to helping white social justice activists become principled and effective anti-racist organizers—both to challenge white privilege and to work for racial justice in all social justice work.

The Mandala Center
www.mandalaforchange.com
(360) 344-3435
A multi-disciplinary education organization dedicated to community dialogue, social justice and personal transformation.

National Women's Alliance
www.nwaforchange.org
(202) 518-5411
A community-driven national advocacy organization dedicated to ending all forms of oppression against women and girls of color.

National Youth Advocacy Coalition
www.nyacyouth.org
(202) 319-7596
A social justice organization that advocates for and with young people who are lesbian, gay, bisexual, transgender or questioning (LGBTQ) in an effort to end discrimination against these youth and to ensure their physical and emotional well being.

The People's Institute for Survival and Beyond
www.thepeoplesinstitute.org
(504) 241-7472
Dedicated to examining history, culture, internal dynamics of leadership and networking to help others face the issue of racism and learn to educate others for 23 years.

SOUL
www.youthec.org/soul/
(510) 451-5466
A training center to develop a new multi-racial generation of young organizers who will have the skills and the vision they need to struggle for the liberation of all oppressed people.

Training for Change
www.trainingforchange.org
(215) 241-7035
Dedicated to helping groups stand up for justice, peace and the environment through strategic non-violence.

Western States Center
www.wscpdx.org
(503) 228-8866
Works to build a progressive movement for social, economic, racial and environmental justice in the eight western states of Oregon, Washington, Idaho, Montana, Wyoming, Utah, Nevada and Alaska.

training in communication and facilitation skills

Public Conversations Project
www.publicconversations.org
(617) 923-1216
Promotes constructive conversations and relationships among people who have differing values, world views and perspectives about divisive public issues.

National Coalition for Dialogue and Deliberation
www.thataway.org
(802) 254-7341
Brings together those who actively practice, promote and study inclusive, high quality conversations.

Interaction Institute for Social Change
www.interactioninstitute.org
(617) 234-2750
Provides individuals with the skills they need to develop personally and professionally and to become catalysts for improving performance, building collaborative cultures and achieving extraordinary results.

Lucy Leu and Marshall B. Rosenberg (eds.), *Nonviolent Communication,* Puddledancer Press, 2003.

fundraising

Changemakers Donor Partner Training
www.changemakers.org/donorprograms.htm
(415) 551-2363
Changemakers works with committed social change donors to foster and advance their leadership, partnership and fundraising skills.

Grassroots Fundraising Journal
www.grassrootsfundraising.org
Offers practical tips and tools to help with raising money for organizations.

Grassroots Institute for Fundraising Training (GIFT)
www.grassrootsinstitute.org
(303) 455-6361
GIFT's mission is to change the color of philanthropy by developing and strengthening the grassroots fundraising skills of individuals and organizations working for social justice, with an emphasis on communities of color.

Kim Klein, *Fundraising for Social Change,* Jossey-Bass, 2000.

Resist, *Finding Funding: A Beginner's Guide to Foundation Research, 5th Edition.*
This online guide to fundraising is a project of Resist, a social change foundation,
and can be downloaded at www.resistinc.org/resources/finding_funding.html.

socially responsible spending

Don't forget to think about who owns the businesses where you spend money.
Most areas have listings like the *Black Pages,* minority and women-owned businesses
divisions at the local Chamber of Commerce and networks of LGBT (lesbian, gay,
bisexual and transgender) business owners.

Fair Trade Federation
www.fairtradefederation.org
An association of fair trade wholesalers, retailers and producers. Includes a directory
of members' stores and on-line shopping sites.

Green Pages
www.greenpages.org
Directory of qualified green businesses with over 25,000 products and services from
2,000 green companies.

Public Citizen
www.publiccitizen.org
A national non-profit consumer advocacy organization.

Simple Living Network
www.simpleliving.net
Provides tools, examples and contacts for conscious, simple,
healthy and restorative living.

Union Label
www.unionlabel.org
Promotes the products and services produced in America by union members

Michael Brower and Warren Leon, *The Consumer's Guide to Effective Environmental
Choices: Practical Advice from the Union of Concerned Scientists,* Three Rivers
Press, 1999.

Ingrid Newkirk, *Making Kind Choices : Everyday Ways to Enhance Your Life
Through Earth- and Animal-Friendly Living,* St. Martin's Griffin, 2005.

John Robbins, *Diet for a New America: How Your Food Choices Affect Your Health, Happiness and the Future of Life on Earth*, H.J. Kramer, 1998.

financial literacy and financial planning

Not all of these sources have a socially responsible investing (SRI) perspective, but they can still help with building financial literacy skills and getting an overview of what financial planning is.

My Money
www.mymoney.gov
It may seem weird, but the federal government has set up a helpful financial literacy site.

The Motley Fool
www.fool.com
This site has some pretty easy to read explanations of how financial planning and investing works.

Co-op America, *Financial Planning Handbook*.
Available at www.coopamerica.org where there's also a ton of other SRI resources.

Joanne Kabak and Rosemary Williams, *A Woman's Book of Money and Spiritual Vision: Putting Your Financial Values into Spiritual Perspective,* Innisfree Press, 2001.

Susan Knox, *Financial Basics: A Money Management Guide for Students,* Ohio State University Press, 2004.

Harold L. Lustig, *4 Steps to Financial Security for Lesbian and Gay Couples,* Ballantine Books, 1999.

Eric Tyson, *Personal Finance for Dummies,* For Dummies, 2003.

socially responsible investing

As You Sow
www.asyousow.org
A non-profit organization dedicated to promoting corporate social responsibility.

Community Development Finance Institutions Coalition
www.cdfi.org

Corpwatch

www.corpwatch.org

CorpWatch counters corporate-led globalization through education, network-building and activism.

Foundation Partnership on Corporate Responsibility

www.foundationpartnership.org

An association of foundations working to link their grantmaking values with their investments.

Green Money Journal

www.greenmoney.com

Focuses on socially and environmentally responsible business, investing and consumer resources.

National Federation of Community Development Credit Unions

www.natfed.org

Shareholder Action Network

www.shareholderaction.org

A clearinghouse of information and analysis for the socially responsible investing community on shareholder advocacy.

Social Funds

www.socialfunds.com

Has information on SRI mutual funds, community investments, corporate research, shareowner actions and daily social investment news.

Social Investment Forum

www.socialinvest.org

A national non-profit organization providing research and educational programs on socially responsible investing.

Social Venture Network

www.svn.org

A progressive business network that offers support for companies that value social justice, community, cooperation, diversity, education, sustainability and innovation.

Responsible Endowments Coalition

www.sriendowment.org

A diverse network of students and alumni from across the country dedicated to advancing socially and environmentally responsible investing in relation to college and university endowments.

Responsible Investing
www.responsibleinvesting.org
A public database containing complete equity holdings and screening categories of SRI mutual funds in the U.S. and Canada.

Hal Brill, *Investing with Your Values: Making Money and Making a Difference,* New Society Publishers, 2000.

Amy L. Domini, *Socially Responsible Investing: Making a Difference and Making Money,* Dearborn Trade, 2001.

Paul Hawken, *The Ecology of Commerce: A Declaration of Sustainability,* HarperBusiness, 1994.

books about giving

Chuck Collins and Pam Rogers with Joan P. Garner, *Robin Hood Was Right: A Guide to Giving Your Money for Social Change,* W.W. Norton & Company, 2001.

Tracy Gary and Melissa Kohner, *Inspired Philanthropy: Your Step-By-Step Guide To Creating a Giving Plan,* Josey Bass, 2002.

Christopher Mogil and Anne Slepian, *Welcome to Philanthropy: Resources for Individuals and Families Exploring Social Change Giving,* National Network of Grantmakers, 1997.

Christopher Mogil and Anne Slepian with Pete Woodrow, *We Gave Away a Fortune,* New Society Publishers, 1992.

books about social change philanthropy

Mark Dowie, *American Foundations: An Investigative History,* MIT Press, 2002.

Pablo Eisenberg and Stacy Palmer, *Challenges For Nonprofits And Philanthropy: The Courage To Change,* Tufts University, 2004.

Ellen Furnari, Carol Mollner, Teresa Odendahl and Aileen Shaw, *Exemplary Grantmaking Practices Manual,* National Network of Grantmakers, 1997. Available at www.nng.org.

John Hunsaker and Brenda Hanzl, *Understanding Social Justice Philanthropy,* National Committee for Responsive Philanthropy, 2003. Available at www.ncrp.org.

Joint Affinity Groups, *Diversity Practices in Foundations: Findings from a National Study,* 2001. Report can be downloaded at www.lgbtfunders.org/lgbtfunders/JAG/diversity_study.htm.

Ellen Condliffe Lagemann (ed.), *Philanthropic Foundations: New Scholarship, New Possibilities,* Indiana University Press, 1999.

Susan Ostrander, *Money for Change: Social Movement Philanthropy at Haymarket People's Fund,* Temple University Press, 1997.

Tides Foundation, *Donor Activist Collaboration: A Potential Vehicle for Promoting Community, Accountability and Effectiveness in Grantmaking,* The Tides Foundation, 2003. Call Tides at (415) 561-6400 to get a copy.

places to learn more about giving and social change philanthropy

Asian Americans/Pacific Islanders in Philanthropy (AAPIP)
www.aapip.org
(415) 273-2760

Changemakers
www.changemakers.org
(415) 551-2363
A national public foundation that models and supports community-based social change philanthropy.

Disability Funders Network
www.disabilityfunders.org
(703) 560-0099

Emerging Practitioners in Philanthropy (EPIP)
www.epip.org
(212) 472-0508
A network of young and emerging grantmakers who are interested in advancing effective social justice philanthropy.

Environmental Grantmakers Association
www.ega.org
(212) 812-4260

Funders for Lesbian and Gay Issues
www.lgbtfunders.org
(212) 475-2930

Funders Network on Trade and Globalization
www.fntg.org
(415) 642-6022

Grantmakers Without Borders
www.internationaldonors.org
(617) 794-2253
A network of foundations and donors committed to expanding global social change philanthropy.

Hispanics in Philanthropy
www.hiponline.org
(415) 837-0427

National Committee for Responsive Philanthropy (NCRP)
www.ncrp.org
(202) 387-9177
A national watchdog, research and advocacy organization that promotes public accountability and accessibility in philanthropy.

National Network of Grantmakers (NNG)
www.nng.org
(612) 724-0702
NNG is a membership network of foundations and individuals involved in funding social and economic justice.

Native Americans in Philanthropy
www.nativephilanthropy.org
(612) 724-8798

Neighborhood Funders Group
www.nfg.org
(202) 833-4690
A network of funders that support community-based efforts that improve economic and social conditions in low-income communities.

Tides Foundation
www.tides.org
(415) 561-6400
Partners with donors to increase and organize resources for positive social change.

Twenty-First Century Foundation
www.21cf.org
(212) 662-3700
A national foundation that supports African American community revitalization, education and leadership development.

Women's Funding Network
www.wfnet.org
(415) 441-0706
A membership organization of more than 90 public and private women's foundations that empower women and girls.

finding activist-led funds

There are many foundations that rely on activist expertise to guide some or all of their grant-making decisions. Unfortunately there's no particular "brand name" for places that believe in this kind of decision-making process. A few of the categories these funds sometimes fall under are: community-based public foundations, women's funds, LGBT (lesbian, gay, bisexual and transgender) foundations, public funds, community foundations and social justice foundations. So you may need to ask a few questions before you can tell whether or not a foundation actually has an activist-led giving process.

Below are only a few examples of some national and international foundations with activist-led giving processes. There are tons more and this doesn't even begin to cover local, regional, issue and identity-based funds. Any of the organizations listed above in the social change philanthropy resources section can help you find out more. Also, there are lists of funds at www.changemakers.org, www.fex.org and www.wfnet.org.

Astraea Lesbian Action Foundation
www.astraea.org
(212) 529-8021

The Funding Exchange
www.fex.org
(212) 529-5300
A network of social justice community funds across the country.

Global Fund for Women
www.globalfundforwomen.org
(415) 202-7640

Global Greengrants Fund
www.greengrants.org
(303) 939-9866

International Development Exchange
www.idex.org
(415) 824-8384

Jewish Fund for Justice
www.jfjustice.org
(212) 213-2113

New World Foundation
www.newwf.org
(212) 249-1023

Peace Development Fund
www.peacefund.org
(413) 256-8306

RESIST, Inc.
www.resistinc.org
(617) 623-5110

Self Education Foundation
www.selfeducation.org

Southern Partners Fund
www.spfund.org
(404) 758-1983

Third Wave Foundation
www.thirdwavefoundation.org
(212) 675-0700

Thank you to our sponsors...

Thank you to our lead sponsor:

Progressive Asset Management • www.pamny.com • (800) 659-8189
Progressive Asset Management/New York (PAM/NY) offers individualized investment services tailored to your specific needs and personal convictions. You can achieve your goals in a socially responsible way when you work with a team of professionals who take the time to understand your values and work to achieve your financial objectives. For our foundation clients we offer financial consulting including investment policy development, asset management, gift processing, cash flow management and charitable giving strategies. Securities are offered through Financial West Group, Inc. Member NASD, SIPC, MSRB.

And to all our sponsors:

Appalachian Community Fund (ACF) • www.appalachiancommunityfund.org • (865) 523-5783
ACF provides grants to groups promoting progressive change in the central region of Appalachia. Grants are given to community-based organizations that address underlying causes of the economic and social distress of the region, and are targeted to organizations and communities with little or no access to other moneys.

Astraea Lesbian Foundation For Justice • www.astraeafoundation.org • (212) 529-8021
The Astraea Lesbian Foundation For Justice works for social, racial and economic justice in the U.S. and internationally. Its grant-making and philanthropic advocacy programs help lesbians and allied communities challenge oppression and claim their human rights. The world's largest lesbian foundation, Astraea is primarily supported by individual members.

Bread and Roses Community Fund • www.breadrosesfund.org • (215) 731-1107
Bread and Roses Community Fund brings together donors and activists who share a vision of a just society, one in which power and resources are distributed equitably. The Fund provides grants and technical assistance to support disenfranchised communities in the Delaware Valley that are taking collective action to bring about economic and social change locally and around the world.

Boston Common Asset Management • www.bostoncommonasset.com • (617) 720-5557
Boston Common Asset Management is a full-service social investment firm dedicated to the pursuit of financial return and social change. We offer large-cap equity and balanced portfolios as well as international and small-cap products. We tailor portfolios to each client's social and financial goals, combining prudent investment management, diligent in-house social research and path-breaking shareholder advocacy.

Calvert Foundation • www.calvertfoundation.org • www.calvertgiving.org • (800) 248-0337
Calvert Foundation is a nonprofit organization that uses your investment capital to create hope and opportunity through a global portfolio of 200 community development and social enterprises. Find out more about the innovative fixed-term and -rate Calvert Community Investment Notes and about the donor advised Calvert Giving Fund at our website or by calling the number above.

Changemakers • www.changemakers.org • (415) 551-2363
Changemakers is a national public foundation that models and supports community-based social

change philanthropy. We work within the philanthropic sector to shift *where* money is directed—to address root causes of social and environmental problems—and *how* it is given, urging individual donors and philanthropic organizations to become more accountable, strategic, inclusive, collaborative, democratic and creative.

Chinook Fund • www.chinookfund.org • (303) 455-6905
Chinook is respected throughout Colorado for its pioneering support of organizations working to ameliorate the root causes of injustice: classism, racism, sexism, homophobia, ableism and ageism. Consistent with Chinook's commitment to supporting organizations that are led by those who are most directly impacted by the policies and programs they seek to change, grant awards are made by its all volunteer, community activist-led grant-making committee.

Crossroads Fund • www.crossroadsfund.org • (773) 227-7676
Crossroads Fund supports community organizations working on issues of social and economic justice in the Chicago area. Since 1981, we have distributed millions of dollars to hundreds of grassroots organizations. Often Crossroads provides the first foundation support for new and emerging groups that grow to gain visibility and create lasting change throughout the city and beyond.

EcoLogic Development Fund • www.ecologic.org • (617) 441-6300
The EcoLogic Development Fund conserves endangered wildlife and wildlands by advancing community-based development and resource management.

The Fund for Santa Barbara • www.fundforsantabarbara.org • (805) 962-9164
The Fund for Santa Barbara is an activist-led community foundation that supports grassroots community groups working for social, economic, environmental and political justice in Santa Barbara County, California. The Fund provides grants and technical assistance to 200 projects each year, and has awarded over $2.8 million since it's founding in 1980.

Fund for Southern Communities (FSC) • www.fundforsouth.org • (404) 371-8404
FSC is a public foundation that supports and unites organizations and donors working to create just and sustainable communities. Through fundraising and grant-making, the Fund has a responsible and effective link between donors and organizations that are working for social change. FSC supports community groups in Georgia, North Carolina and South Carolina.

Funding Exchange • www.fex.org • (212) 529-5300
The Funding Exchange is a national network of publicly supported, community-based foundations. We are a unique partnership of activists and donors dedicated to building a base of support for progressive social, racial, political and economic change. The network collectively raises and distributes 15 million dollars annually through local, national and international grant-making programs.

The Global Fund for Women • www.globalfundforwomen.org • (415) 202-7640
The Global Fund for Women is a grantmaking organization committed to a world of equality and social justice. We make grants to seed, support and link women's rights groups based outside the U.S. working to address critical issues such as gaining economic independence, increasing girls access to education and stopping violence against women.

Haymarket People's Fund • www.haymarket.org • (617) 522-7676

Haymarket People's Fund is a progressive foundation that funds grassroots social change groups throughout New England. Haymarket was founded in 1974 by young people with inherited wealth who wanted to fund "change, not charity." Haymarket engages donors in social change through workshops, conferences, anti-racist trainings, donor-advised philanthropy and other programs.

Investors' Circle (IC) • www.investorscircle.net • (617) 566-2600

IC is one of the nation's oldest and largest angel investor networks. Its 130 members have invested over $100 million in private companies and venture funds devoted to solving major social and environmental problems.

MADRE • www.madre.org • (212) 627-0444

MADRE is an international women's human rights organization that works in partnership with women's community-based groups in conflict zones to address issues of health, education, economic development and other human rights. MADRE partnerships enable our sister organizations to meet concrete needs while working to promote long-term development and social justice.

Ms. Foundation for Women • www.ms.foundation.org • (212) 742-2300

The Ms. Foundation for Women is the first and leading national women's philanthropy. We provide grants and practical training to U.S. based activist women's organizations, empowering them to drive social change and public policy advances in health and safety, economic security, and women's and girls' leadership.

The New World Foundation • www.newwf.org • (212) 249-1023

The New World Foundation supports organizations working to strengthen and expand civil rights and the active participation of citizens in American democracy. Our strategy is to support the building of social movements by supporting organizing, which builds a sustainable mass base of activists in viable organizations.

NorthStar Asset Management • www.northstarasset.com • (617) 522-2635

NorthStar balances clients' social and political concerns with their financial objectives. With individual attention, we examine the financial and social impact of your investments offering tools for action: shareholder action, strategic giving and divestment. At NorthStar, being wealthy and politically engaged is not an oxymoron; rather, it is encouraged, nurtured and praised.

North Star Fund • www.northstarfund.org • (212) 620-9110

The North Star Fund is one of New York City's leading community foundations working to ensure a more equitable and democratic city for all New Yorkers. North Star achieves this mission by organizing donors and raising money for grants that support activism which addresses both the underlying causes and visible manifestations of poverty, racism, homophobia and gender discrimination.

Peace Development Fund • www.peacedevelopmentfund.org • (413) 256-8306

The Peace Development Fund is a public foundation providing grants and other resources to strengthen a broad-based social justice movement that embodies and honors many cultures to build a peaceful, just and equitable world. The grassroots groups we support channel the power of marginalized communities toward fundamental social transformation.

Proteus Fund • www.proteusfund.org • (413) 256-0349
A public foundation established in 1994, Proteus Fund supports statewide and grassroots organizations that are building a national movement for democracy and civic participation. Through a range of innovative and strategic philanthropy programs and services, Proteus helps donors support long-term change to advance social justice and the common good.

Rudolph Steiner Foundation (RSF) • www.rsfoundation.org • (415) 561-3900
RSF is a leader in the emerging field of social finance. RSF supports projects solving some of the world's most pressing problems. With a focus on environmental, economic and social sustainability, RSF offers philanthropic and advisory services to individuals and institutions. RSF's investment fund makes loans directly to organizations providing social benefit.

San Diego Foundation for Change • www.foundation4change.org • (619) 692-0527
The mission of the San Diego Foundation for Change is to fund and support community-led efforts which promote social equality, economic justice, and environmental sustainability. We promote positive, permanent change in the San Diego/Tijuana border region.

Southern Partners Fund (SPF) • www.spfund.org • (404) 758-1983
SPF is a public foundation created to serve Southern communities and organizations seeking social, economic and environmental justice by providing them with financial resources, technical assistance and access to systems of information and power. SPF makes grants for general operating and capacity building as well as travel, technical assistance and discretionary awards.

Third Wave Foundation • www.thirdwavefoundation.org • (212) 675-0700
Third Wave Foundation is a feminist, activist foundation working nationally to support young women 15 to 30. Through financial resources, technical assistance, public education and relationship building, Third Wave helps support and strengthen young women and their allies working for gender, racial, social and economic justice.

Threshold Foundation • www.thresholdfoundation.org • (415) 561-6400
Threshold is a community of individuals united through wealth and a progressive foundation mobilizing money, people and power to create a more just, joyful and sustainable world. Threshold Foundation serves the social change movement through collaborating with and funding innovative U.S.-based and international nonprofit organizations and individuals working towards social justice, environmental sustainability, humane economic systems and peaceful coexistence.

Tides Foundation • www.tidesfoundation.org • (415) 561-6400
For 30 years, Tides Foundation has worked with individual donors, families and institutional grant-makers committed to positive social change. We offer donor-advised funds, expert philanthropic advice and full grantmaking services. We are a mission driven organization committed to promoting human rights, economic justice and a healthy, sustainable environment.

The Twenty-First Century Foundation (21CF) • www.21cf.org • (212) 662-3700
The mission of 21CF is to advance strategic Black philanthropy. Since 1971, 21CF's grants programs have supported more than 350 Black community-based organizations focusing on economic empowerment, leadership development and building community capacity to ensure equal access to jobs, education and other resources for the African American community in the U.S.

Trillium Asset Management • www.trilliuminvest.com • (617) 423-6655

Trillium Asset Management Corporation is the oldest and largest independent investment management firm in the U.S. devoted exclusively to socially responsible investing. Since 1982 individuals and institutions have chosen to invest with Trillium Asset Management because of our emphasis on personalized service, an investment discipline providing consistent and competitive returns and the unique focus on social research and advocacy.

Wisconsin Community Fund (WCF) • www.wcfund.org • (608) 251-6834

WCF is a public foundation that has been supporting grassroots social justice organizations throughout Wisconsin since 1982. Our mission is to raise funds and award grants to progressive groups working for human rights, economic justice, environmental protection and peace. WCF is a member of the Funding Exchange, a national network of 15 funds headquartered in New York City.

Women Donors Network (WDN) • www.womendonors.org • (650) 855-9600

WDN, a national network of women, is a progressive philanthropic community. WDN unites powerful, visionary women committed to social and environmental justice through activism and grantmaking. Activities include an annual conference, study circles, collaborative funding opportunities and philanthropic skill-building. Our intimate community is a safe and caring environment to explore all issues of philanthropy.

about the authors

Karen Pittelman has worked with Resource Generation for the last five years and served as RG's first Program Coordinator. At 25 she dissolved her $3 million trust fund to co-found the Chahara Foundation, a fund run by and for low-income women activists in Boston. She's now 30 and living and writing in her hometown of New York City.

Molly Hein is a multi-media artist whose work creates dialogue across borders and encourages people to examine their relationships to race and class privilege. She brings her background in documentary video, graffiti art and community organizing to her illustrations for *Classified*. She is a 27-year-old New York City native currently living in Minneapolis. Check out more of her work at www.mollyhein.com.

Resource Generation is a national non-profit organization that works with young people with wealth who believe in social change. RG offers programs that support and challenge participants to align their resources with their values. RG is located in Boston and led by a cross-class board and staff.